Canadian Residents'
RHEUMATOLOGY Handbook

Edited by Lori Albert, M. D.
Post-graduate Education Working Group,
Canadian Rheumatology Association

2005
First Edition

Endorsed by

Canadian Rheumatology Association
Société Canadienne de Rhumatologie

Note for Librarians: A cataloguing record for this book is available from Library and Archives Canada at www.collectionscanada.ca/amicus/index-e.html

ISBN 1-4120-5919-4

Printed in Victoria, BC, Canada. Printed on paper with minimum 30% recycled fibre. Trafford's print shop runs on "green energy" from solar, wind and other environmentally-friendly power sources.

TRAFFORD
PUBLISHING

Offices in Canada, USA, Ireland and UK

This book was published *on-demand* in cooperation with Trafford Publishing. On-demand publishing is a unique process and service of making a book available for retail sale to the public taking advantage of on-demand manufacturing and Internet marketing. On-demand publishing includes promotions, retail sales, manufacturing, order fulfilment, accounting and collecting royalties on behalf of the author.

Book sales for North America and international:
Trafford Publishing, 6E–2333 Government St.,
Victoria, BC v8t 4p4 CANADA
phone 250 383 6864 (toll-free 1 888 232 4444)
fax 250 383 6804; email to orders@trafford.com
Book sales in Europe:
Trafford Publishing (uk) Ltd., Enterprise House, Wistaston Road Business Centre,
Wistaston Road, Crewe, Cheshire cw2 7rp UNITED KINGDOM
phone 01270 251 396 (local rate 0845 230 9601)
facsimile 01270 254 983; orders.uk@trafford.com
Order online at:
trafford.com/05-0820

10 9 8 7 6 5 4 3 2

The contents of the **Canadian Residents' Rheumatology Handbook** are to be used as a guide only, and health care professionals should use sound clinical judgment and individualize therapy to each specific patient care situation. This book is sold without warranties of any kind, express or implied, and the publisher, reviewers, and author disclaim any liability, loss, or damage caused by the contents.

This publication reflects the views and experience of the authors, and not necessarily those of Pfizer.

The development of this book has been made possible by an unrestricted educational grant from Pfizer Canada.

Graphic Design & Layout by Fatema Mullan

Acknowledgements

I would like to acknowledge the Post-graduate Education Working Group of the CRA, and the other contributors to this Handbook, for their hard work and support in bringing this book to fruition. Our group first met in 2001 and continues to work together to improve learning opportunities in rheumatology for internal medicine trainees.

I would also like to acknowledge the incredible work of Fatema Mullan - office assistant by day and layout designer by night. Her tremendous dedication to this project helped it to become a reality.

Finally, I want to acknowledge and thank The Arthritis Society for their enduring support. The opportunity to hold a Clinician-Teacher award from TAS made it possible for me to initiate and develop this project. I am grateful for their significant support for medical education.

> \- Lori Albert MD FRCPC
> April 2005

To   JY, H and E

Why You Should Consider Rheumatology as a Career

I chose rheumatology as a career during my Internal Medicine training. I was influenced by the rheumatologists with whom I worked. They were mentors in issues related to medicine as well as being well-rounded and family centered. I found the patients interesting, both in terms of physical findings and the immunology that precipitated the clinical manifestations. There were also tremendous opportunities to do research. Rheumatology is primarily an ambulatory specialty, and I have found that. I am able to strike a balance in my life, with time for my family, my clinical practice and my research. I am very happy and challenged with my career choice.

> *Janet Pope, MD, MPH, FRCPC*
> Associate Professor of Medicine, St. Joseph's Health Care, University of Western Ontario

I decided on rheumatology as a career during my PGY1 year. I decided that a community practice model was my goal, while maintaining an academic relationship with U of T. This was supported by my mentors and they helped me to develop a knowledge base, clinical skill set and habits that would serve my community and my patients well.

Over the past 24 years, maintaining relationships with mentors and new colleagues, including allied health professionals , has allowed me to be involved in the development of an exciting new model for Interdisciplinary Care for patients with arthritis, which has evolved into a Regional program. I continue to teach at all levels, including medical students, rheumatology trainees and allied health professionals.

Rheumatology has never left me disappointed - Intellectually challenging, rewarding relationships with patients and colleagues, successful and gratifying therapies!

> *Carter Thorne MD, FRCPC. FACP*
> Medical Director of the Arthritis Program, Consultant Southlake Regional Health Center, Ontario

I enjoy most facets of medicine. Thus when choosing a career in medicine, a multi-disciplinary specialty which interacted with most clinical disciplines, and also afforded the opportunity to sustain long term, ongoing relationships with patients was of utmost importance. It is for these reasons that I selected rheumatology.

I decided to pursue research and elected to develop an expertise in genetic epidemiology. This was an emerging area of study in rheumatology and I had a unique opportunity to access an enriched founder population, which likely has a high genetic burden for complex rheumatic diseases. With many hours in the clinic, wards, and lab, coupled with invaluable mentoring and many fruitful collaborations, all this hard work recently paid off as my clinical and research endeavors led me to be nominated as one of Canada's Top 40 under 40 for 2003.

Proton Rahman, MD, FRCPC
Associate Professor of Medicine, Memorial University of Newfoundland

I have practiced rheumatology for the past 16 years in a busy community practice. What opened my eyes to Rheumatology was the mix of fascinating diseases rheumatologists deal with every day. I continue to believe rheumatology is the most rewarding and interesting of all the Internal medicine subspecialties.

Rheumatology practice is primarily office based which allows me to control my daily schedule and make time available for activities outside of work which are important for a healthy lifestyle. During my years in practice, I have been able to balance having a very busy practice with having a family (I have 2 sons) and staying physically fit (I have trained for and run 4 marathons, including Boston).

Even after 16 years, almost every day I see patients with the most unusual and challenging problems in my office. It is also immensely rewarding to see an acutely ill young woman with SLE go into remission. New treatments for rheumatoid arthritis have changed the face of this disease and have made a huge impact on our ability to treat people effectively. Indeed, it is now the most interesting time in history to be a rheumatologist.

Jacqueline Stewart MD, FRCPC
Rheumatologist, Penticton Regional Hospital, BC

TABLE OF CONTENTS

Section 1. INTRODUCTION

Section 2. "APPROACH TO..." COMMON RHEUMATIC PRESENTATIONS

SECTION 3. APPROACH TO SELECTION AND INTERPRETATION OF LABORATORY TESTS IN RHEUMATIC DISEASES

Section 4. APPROACH TO THERAPEUTICS

Section 5. SELECTED RHEUMATOLOGIC EMERGENCIES

TABLE OF CONTENTS (CONTINUED)

[Section 1]
Introduction

Introduction to the Rheumatology Curriculum
Dr. Lori Albert, University of Toronto

Welcome to Rheumatology!

Rheumatology is a subspecialty of internal medicine that deals with an array of fascinating inflammatory and autoimmune conditions as well as more common, but often disabling painful musculoskeletal conditions. Virtually every subspecialty in medicine features organ specific manifestations or complications of rheumatic disease. Likewise, rheumatology is a microcosm of the spectrum of general internal medicine.

This handbook has been put together by a post-graduate education Working Group affiliated with the Canadian Rheumatology Association . We have developed a rheumatology curriculum for core medicine residents across Canada to ensure that every resident leaving the post-graduate training program is confident and competent in identifying and initiating management of common rheumatologic problems. This manual is the first part of the "course materials" that will provide you with some of the tools you need to help you achieve these goals.

How to Use This Manual

Please familiarize yourself with the general objectives for your rheumatology training found in the next section. These are meant to help guide your learning in rheumatology over the next 3 years.

The remainder of the manual contains concise chapters on the "Critical" Content of the rheumatology curriculum. The chapters are not exhaustive reviews of each topic, but rather, practical information that will be useful in the clinical settings of ward, ambulatory clinic and emergency department. These chapters are also meant to stimulate your interest and further reading on these topics, as they arise during your clinical experience over the next 3 years. Many chapters will have a short reading list or relevant references in the literature to which you can turn for more depth. Other excellent sources for more detailed reading include:

Kelley's Textbook of Rheumatology, 7th ed., Harris ED, Jr, Budd RC, Firestein GS, et al, (Eds). WB Saunders, Philadelphia 2005.

Rheumatology, 3rd ed., Hochberg MC, Silman AJ, Smolen JS, Weinblatt ME, Weisman MH, (Eds). Mosby, St. Louis 2003

Primer on the Rheumatic Diseases, 12th ed., Klippel JH ed. Altlanta, USA: Arthritis Foundation, 2001

Up to Date©

Recommended Journals include The New England Journal of Medicine, Annals of Internal Medicine, JAMA, Arthritis and Rheumatism, and The Journal of Rheumatology.

Other important information and links can be found at:

Canadian Rheumatology Association website www.cra.ucalgary.ca

American College of Rheumatology website www.rheumatology.org

A "checklist" has been included to help you monitor your progress through the curriculum.

There is also space designated as a "case log" to help you record rheumatology cases that you see during your training and the "pearls" you glean from managing these cases.

Keep your manual handy - you will have cause to use it many times over the next three years!

GENERAL OBJECTIVES

1. Recognize and have familiarity with management of common rheumatic diseases, with the goal of early diagnosis to minimize morbidity and mortality.

2. Enhance expertise in history taking and physical examination relevant to the clinical problems of monoarthritis, polyarthritis, multisystem disease and regional/generalized pain problems.

3. Learn the appropriate use and interpretation of tests in clinical immunology and diagnostic imaging to facilitate diagnosis of rheumatic diseases.

4. Develop a systematic approach to the initial /emergency therapy of patients having rheumatic disease. This includes developing an appreciation of when referral to a rheumatologist would optimize patient management.

CRITICAL CONTENT

Knowledge

A.
- ▶ Approach to diagnosis and management of acute monoarthritis
- ▶ Approach to diagnosis and management of acute and chronic polyarthritis
- ▶ Approach to the patient who "hurts all over"
- ▶ Approach to acute and chronic back pain
- ▶ Approach to regional pain disorders (shoulder, knee, ankle)
- ▶ Approach to osteoarthritis
- ▶ Approach to rheumatoid arthritis
- ▶ Approach to systemic vasculitis
- ▶ Approach to collagen vascular disease
- ▶ Rheumatic manifestations of medical diseases
- ▶ Rheumatic manifestations of HIV disease
- ▶ Approach to osteoporosis

B. Approach to selection and interpretation of laboratory tests in rheumatic diseases

C. Essential therapeutics (Approach to treatment and specific drugs)

D. Rheumatologic emergencies

Skills

A. MSK screening exam
B. Detailed joint exam
C. Selected joint aspiration and injection techniques

POINTS OF ACCESS FOR LEARNING

In addition to self-learning through this manual, textbooks and web-based media there are a number of activities that will be available to you for meeting the learning objectives laid out above.

In most centres, the Department of Medicine will offer a series of seminars/lectures encompassing important topics in the subspecialties. Rheumatology lectures will be included in this and usually cover the key content topics outlined above. "Morning report" is often a forum in which rheumatology cases are discussed. Some centres will have academic half-days that include rheumatology ambulatory care. Finally, your rotation on rheumatology will give you the best opportunity to learn about the rheumatic diseases through enriched exposure to common rheumatic problems as well as more complex and challenging cases. Most rheumatology divisions offer a variety of learning activities and divisional rounds. If you are interested in attending these sessions when you are not on the rotation, speak to the education coordinator for your rheumatology center.

[Section 2]

"Approach To..."
Common Rheumatic
Presentations

[1] Approach to Monoarthritis
Dr. Doug Smith, University of Ottawa

KEY CONCEPTS

Pain and swelling of a single joint (monoarthritis) is often a process that develops acutely. There are important features of the history and physical examination that can help to narrow the differential diagnosis, and occasionally be diagnostic. If trauma is excluded as a cause, in most cases the diagnosis will fall into one of three groups of conditions:

▶ Infections - most important to diagnose and treat quickly!

▶ Crystals (gout or pseudogout)

▶ Seronegative spondyloarthropathies (reactive arthritis, psoriatic, enteropathic.)

The process of developing a differential includes the following key concepts:

1. Is there a history of trauma?

2. Decide if the process is articular or non-articular.

3. Use clues from the history and physical to narrow the differential diagnosis (age, gender, risk factors, previous episodes, family history, back pain, travel history). The presence of extra-articular manifestations is particularly helpful.

4. Laboratory data may be supportive, but generally cannot be used to establish the diagnosis.

5. Aspiration and analysis of synovial fluid is necessary to firmly establish the diagnosis and guide therapy.

HISTORY

Patient Demographics

- ▶ **Any age:** think of infectious causes
- ▶ **Young men/women:** Think of infection and also seronegative spondyloarthropathies (reactive, psoriatic or enteropathic.) Remember, young women don't get gout!
- ▶ **Older men/women:** Think of infection and also crystals.

Key Questions

In order to narrow down your diagnosis:

1. Is there a history of trauma?
2. Is this the first episode of acute joint inflammation?
3. Is this truly an articular process or is it non-articular/periarticular?
4. Is there a history of risk factors for STDs, travel or other infections?
5. Is there axial (spinal) involvement
6. Look for helpful extra-articular features

1. Is there a history of trauma?

- ▶ An acute injury to a joint such as the knee may lead to a hemarthrosis, particularly if there is a meniscal and/or cruciate tear. Trauma may also play a role in periarticular conditions such as olecranon or prepatellar bursitis.

2. Is this the first episode of acute joint inflammation?

- ▶ Recurrent episodes are more suggestive of crystals or seronegative spondyloarthropathies.

3. Is this truly an articular process or is it non-articular/periarticular?

- ▶ Periarticular inflammation may be confused with septic arthritis.
- ▶ In olecranon bursitis the inflammatory process begins in the bursa and may extend to the soft tissues around the elbow. Extension of the elbow is relatively preserved in bursitis, whereas extension is lost early in an acute inflammation of the joint itself.
- ▶ In prepatellar bursitis the inflammatory process begins in the bursa in front of the patella and extends to the soft tissues around the knee. Extension of the knee is relatively preserved, whereas extension is lost early in an acute inflammation of the joint itself.
- ▶ Periarticular inflammation of the ankles, when combined with erythema nodosum is suggestive of acute sarcoidosis.

4. How did it come on?

▶ Gradual and insidious onset:
  ▸▸ Typical for early onset of inflammatory arthritis such as Psoriatic Arthritis

▶ Acute onset:
  ▸▸ Typical for infection, crystals
  ▸▸ Typical of reactive arthritis with history of time lag after a precipitating GI or GU infection.

5. What Joints are involved?

▶ Septic arthritis most commonly occurs due to hematogenous spread of organisms from site of primary infection. Joints affected tend to be medium to large, often weight-bearing and particularly those that have been previously damaged.

▶ Gout tends to involve the 1st MTP, ankle, knee. In older women may affect DIP joints of hands with tophi superimposed on Heberden's nodes (OA.)

▶ Pseudogout commonly presents as an acute monoarthritis affecting a knee or wrist in older individuals.

▶ Seronegative spondyloarthropathies: (see chapter on Approach to Polyarthritis)
  ▸▸ Asymmetrical, lower extremity, larger joints (knees, ankles)
  ▸▸ Enthesitis (inflammation of insertion of tendon and ligament into bone)
    ▹▸ Achilles, plantar fasciitis common (causes of "heel pain").
  ▸▸ Dactylitis (inflammation of tendon sheath producing "sausage digit.")
    ▹▸ Think Psoriatic Arthritis or Reactive Arthritis

▶ The presence of axial involvement suggests a seronegative spondyloarthropathy.

▶ Inflammatory back involvement is characterized by:
  ▸▸ Insidious onset
  ▸▸ Low back/buttock pain, often worse with inactivity
  ▸▸ Prolonged morning stiffness
  ▸▸ Pain relieved by activity

6. Is there a history of risk factors for STDs, Lyme disease or other infections?

▶ Unprotected sex, multiple partners

► Intravenous drug use
► Travel to Lyme endemic areas
  ▸ Tick-born zoonosis caused by Borrelia burgdorferi and transmitted most commonly by blacklegged tick, *Ixodes scapularis*.
  ▸ Endemic in northeastern USA (Maine to Maryland,) Great Lakes region and Midwest USA including Wisconsin and Minnesota and western USA including northern California and Oregon. Also present in Canada and Europe.
  ▸ In Canada, vector ticks sometimes infected with B burgdorferi reported in many provinces but found particularly in two localized regions - along north shore of Lake Erie (Point Pelee, Rondeau Provincial Park) and in Fraser delta, Gulf Islands and Vancouver Island where the vector is Ixodes pacificus.
► Immunosuppression

7. Do you have any symptoms outside of the joints (extra-articular features?)?

► Fever suggests infection but is also seen with other causes, particularly crystals.
► Extra-articular features of seronegative spondyloarthropathies include: oral ulcers, conjunctivitis, uveitis, GU symptoms, GI symptoms, psoriatic rash, keratoderma blenorrhagicum (multiple papular/vesicular lesions on the sole of the foot), circinate balanitis (shallow painless ulcers on the glans penis), enthesitis, dactylitis
► Urethritis/cervicitis, pustular skin lesions, tenosynovitis with disseminated gonococcal infection
► Acute diarrheal illness - reactive (post-dysenteric) arthritis.
► Travel, tick bite, erythematous rash (erythema migrans with Lyme disease.) **Erythema migrans** (Lyme disease) - slowly expanding erythematous lesion beginning at site of tick bite. May have prominent red border with central clearing. Present at some time in course of disease in 80% of patients. Usually associated with nonspecific symptoms such as fever, malaise, headache, myalgia and arthralgia.
► Early dissemination may result in multiple erythema migrans lesions as well as manifestations affecting the nervous system (lymphocytic meningitis, cranial neuropathy especially facial nerve and radiculoneuritis,) and heart (rare transient A-V block.)

in addition to migratory joint and muscle pain.

► Late disseminated disease (weeks to months after infection) most commonly manifests as **intermittent arthritis of one or a few large joints, particularly the knee.** Late neurologic manifestations include chronic axonal polyneuropathy and chronic encephalomyelitis.

8. *Other medical illnesses?*

- ► Inflammatory bowel disease (think enteropathic arthritis)
- ► Psoriasis (think psoriatic arthritis)
- ► Iritis/uveitis (think seronegative, HLAB27 associated diseases)
- ► Recent symptoms of infection, particularly
  - ⇒ GU (think gonococcal and/or post-venereal reactive arthritis.)
  - ⇒ GI (think post-dysenteric reactive arthritis)

9. *Family history?*

- ► Seronegative arthritis, psoriasis, IBD

10. *Medications?*

- ► Medications tried and response (e.g. anti-inflammatories, antibiotics)
- ► Medications used for other reasons - examples;
  - ⇒ gout exacerbated by diuretic use, low dose ASA, cyclosporine...
  - ⇒ Prolonged steroid use leading to avascular necrosis
  - ⇒ anticoagulants and hemarthrosis.

11. *Previous Investigations?*

- ► What if any blood work/imaging studies have been done that might give clues?

12. *Social History*?

- ► Alcohol use
- ► Sexual history, contacts

PHYSICAL EXAMNINATION

Vitals: Look for fever, tachycardia (signs of possible sepsis).

Head and Neck: ocular inflammation (think seronegative spondyloarthropathy) oral ulcers (painless with reactive arthritis, painful with enteropathic arthritis).

Chest: possible source of disseminated infection, crackles (apical fibrosis with spondyloarthropathies) chest expansion as part of spine exam.

CVS: murmurs (aortic insufficiency with long-standing spondyloarthropathies).

Skin and nails:

- ► Psoriasis, nail pitting, onycholysis (think psoriatic arthritis)
- ► Pustular skin lesions (think disseminated gonococcal infection)
- ► Nodules (think tophi/gout)
- ► Lesions on palms and soles (think pustular psoriasis/keratoderma=Reiter's)
- ► Lesions on glans penis (think circinate balanitis=Reiter's)
- ► Erythema nodosum (think enteropathic arthritis, acute sarcoidosis)
- ► Erythema migrans (Lyme Disease)

Neurologic: encephalopathy, neuropathy with Lyme disease.

MSK:

- ► Signs of inflammation such as erythema, warmth, swelling/effusion
- ► Acutely inflamed joints usually have limited range of movement in all planes
- ► Pain and loss of extension typical of synovial inflammation/capsular distension, particularly in elbow, hip and knee
- ► Look for signs of joint effusion. In the elbow swelling due to an effusion is most apparent in the area **between** the olecranon process and the lateral epicondyle. In the knee, a significant effusion produces swelling and distention of the suprapatellar pouch but generally does not extend anterior to the patella
- ► Is inflammation periarticular (e.g. olecranon bursitis, prepatellar bursitis) or articular? With acute joint inflammation swelling/erythema confined by joint capsule and does **not** extend over olecranon process or patella
- ► In a deep joint such as the hip, you may not be able to appreciate classic signs of inflammation. Acute pain and loss of active and passive range of motion may be the only indicators
- ► Look for additional sites of joint involvement of which patient may be unaware. Use the **joint distribution** for diagnostic clues (see chapter 2)
- ► Assess for spine involvement particularly in young-middle aged individuals when seronegative spondyloarthropathies likely to present: SI joint tenderness, loss of lumbar lordosis, Schober test and reduced chest expansion (see section on physical examination in back pain)

LABORATORY INVESTIGATIONS

CBC: look for leukocytosis, left shift as evidence of infection (not very reliable...)

ESR: not specific, but may support a more systemic inflammatory process

Creatinine, LFTs, urinalysis: screening prior to therapy

Serum urate: NOT very helpful during acute attack. Up to 1/3 of patients with acute gout have normal uric acid levels during the acute attack, possibly related to deposition of uric acid in tissues (cartilage, synovium, tophi). A fall in uric acid due to deposition or to use of uric acid lowering medications may precipitate an acute attack by encouraging dissolution of tophaceous deposits.

Cultures: blood, urine, synovial other sites when infection to be ruled out.

Joint Aspiration and Synovial Fluid Analysis:

- ▶ Appearance: blood (hemarthrosis) inflammatory - yellow, turbulent, purulent
- ▶ Cell count, differential - distinguish normal, non-inflammatory, inflammatory, and septic. See table below. These are guidelines only!
- ▶ Gram stain, C&S
- ▶ Crystals:
    - ▶▶ Uric acid: long, thin, needle-shaped, may be in fluid and/or phagocytosed (piercing through) WBCs. Polarize brightly. Strongly negatively birefringent (parallel yellow, perpendicular blue).
    - ▶▶ Pyrophosphate: much smaller, broader, rhomboid shaped, may be in fluid and/or phagocytosed inside WBCs. Polarize weakly (less bright). Weakly positively birefringent (parallel blue, perpendicular yellow).
    - ▶▶ NB: injected steroids appear as tiny pleomorphic crystals, which polarize brightly with intense negative or positive birefringence. Transient post-injection "flares" may be related to these crystals.
    - ▶▶ NB: Gout and septic arthritis may coexist!

	Normal	Non-inflammatory E.g. osteoarthritis	Inflammatory E.g. RA, crystals, spondyloarthropathies	Septic
Appearance	Clear	Clear	Yellow, turbid	Opaque
Viscosity	High	High	Low	Low
Total WBC/mm^3	<200	2000-10,000	5000-75,000	>50,000
% PMNs	<25	<50	>50	>75

Suspect Lyme Disease: (clinical picture, endemic area, tick bite, history of rash)

▶ ELISA + western blot demonstration of antibody response to B. burgdorferi interpreted according to Center for Disease Control guidelines. (NB. After 1 month of disease, majority of patients have positive IgG responses. For acute disease less than 1 month duration sensitivity is low and testing should include both acute and convalescent serum samples.)

IMAGING

Plain radiographs:

▶ Consider affected + contralateral joint for comparison: may be helpful with chondrocalcinosis, unsuspected fracture, osteonecrosis, osteomyelitis, and adjacent bone tumor.

▶ Consider X-rays of SI joints and lumbar spine if seronegative disease is suspected

DIFFERENTIAL DIAGNOSIS

▶ Selected causes of an ACUTE, RED, HOT JOINT:

Infections	Bacteria - Staph aureus most common overall. Hemolytic strep, gram negatives (particularly elderly, underlying disease) H. influenza (kids) Neisseria Mycobacteria Lyme Disease Viral
Crystals	Gout Pseudogout (CPPD) Hydroxyapatite (acute calcific periarthritis)
Traumatic	Hemarthrosis
Spondyloarthropathies	Psoriatic arthritis Reactive arthritis (post-venereal, post dysenteric)
Others	Hemarthrosis 2° trauma, bleeding disorder anticoagulation Palindromic rheumatism Bacterial endocarditis

▶ Selected causes of a more CHRONIC MONOARTHRITIS:

Infections	Mycobacteria Fungi Lyme disease Bacterial
Inflammatory	Spondyloarthropathies- psoriatic, reactive, IBD associated Juvenile chronic arthritis Foreign body synovitis
Non-inflammatory	- Osteoarthritis: sometimes see episodes of more acute inflammation. Also, gout may produce acute red, hot joints +/- tophaceous deposits superimposed on Heberden's, Bouchard's nodes, particularly in older women - Osteonecrosis/avascular necrosis - Hemarthrosis
Tumours	Pigmented Villonodular synovitis
" Idiopathic "	Define as inflammatory or non-inflammatory. May declare itself over time.

INITIAL THERAPY

▶ Decisions regarding **initial** therapy of a patient with a monoarthritis are made in the context of a complete history, physical examination and the results of initial investigations as outlined above. This should almost always include results of synovial fluid appearance, cell count and differential, crystals and gram stain. All appropriate fluids should be cultured at the outset, but will not be back in time to help with the initial treatment decision.

▶ Armed with this information, what is the most likely diagnosis (which should guide initial therapy) and what is the differential diagnosis?

▶ Most commonly, the differential diagnosis will fall into one of the following categories - trauma, infection, crystals or a spondyloarthropathy.

▶ The only significant **contraindication to a joint aspiration** is if there is evidence of infection in the needle path superficial to the joint (e.g. cellulitis, potentially septic bursitis in which case aspiration should be of bursa and not underlying joint.)

▶ Patients with a monoarthritis affecting a **prosthetic joint** should be referred immediately to orthopedics for aspiration and further management.

▶ Non-pharmacologic therapy should include rest, splinting and ice packs to help reduce pain. Physiotherapy should begin when acute situation is beginning to settle.

1. **Trauma:** In general the history is obvious. A significant joint effusion, particularly in the knee, will be a hemarthrosis associated with a potentially significant internal derangement. These patients usually would be referred to orthopedics

2. Suspect infection (see section 5:12):

▶ If **N. gonorrhea** infection suspected (contact, urethritis/cervicitis, pustular skin lesions, arthritis, tenosynovitis) begin therapy with parenteral ceftriaxone (ciproflaoxacin if allergic) Need to be aware of patterns of antibiotic resistance. Because of high rate of transmission of other STDs, recommendation is to treat as well for Chlamydia trachomatis with a single oral dose of azithromycin (alternatives doxycycline or erytromycin X 7 days). All patients should be screened for syphilis and HIV. Contacts also require screening.

▶ If **non-gonococcal septic arthritis** suspected, begin therapy with parenteral cloxacillin to cover most common gram positives and/or cefuroxime for gram-negative coverage. Consider patterns of antibiotic resistance (specifically methicillin-resistant staph aureus). Joint should be aspirated daily and consideration given to orthopedic assessment for lavage/debridement.

▶ **Lyme Disease:** Particularly in early stages readily curable with oral antibiotics such as doxycycline or ampicillin X 14-21 days. Alternatives include cefuroxime or erythromycin. Later involvement with arthritis, neurologic cardiac manifestations may require intravenous therapy.

3. Suspect crystals:

▶ Consider intra-articular steroid injection

▶ If no contraindication, give full dose of an NSAID for +/- 2 weeks

▶ Do **NOT** administer uric acid lowering drugs (e.g. allopurinol), which may precipitate an attack or make the patient worse during an acute attack. Consideration of prescription of uric acid lowering drugs should ONLY occur when the acute attack has completely settled. Indications for use of agents such as allopurinol may include frequent recurrent attacks, tophi, renal disease, kidney stones. Because of the risk of precipitating an acute attack, patients initiating allopurinol therapy need prophylaxis, typically with an NSAID or colchicine 0.6mg once or twice daily for three to six months.

- ► Colchicine:
  - ⇉ Most effective if given early in course of acute attack (< 12-24 hours).
  - ⇉ **Avoid** in patients with significant renal impairment.
  - ⇉ **Particularly useful** in patents in whom NSAIDs contraindicated (peptic ulcer disease, congestive heart failure.)
  - ⇉ Oral, 0.6mg Q2 hours begins to improvement or evidence of toxicity (nausea or diarrhea.) Usually 3-4 doses in first 24 hours.
  - ⇉ Intravenous, 1mg diluted, into free flowing line with care to avoid extravasation. May repeat once in 6 hours if no improvement (this is now rarely used due to potential toxicity).
  - ⇉ Very useful in prophylaxis for patients with recurrent attacks, patients initiating therapy with uric acid lowering drugs (dose 0.6mg once-twice daily with normal renal function).
- ► Corticosteroids:
  - ⇉ **Particularly useful** in complicated medical patient with underlying renal, hepatic and/or cardiac disease.
  - ⇉ Intra-articular, very useful in treatment of monoarticular acute attacks.
  - ⇉ Systemic: Oral prednisone 30-50mg daily and taper over 7-10 days. Intravenous methylprednisolone (or equivalent), 80mg acutely and taper or switch to oral prednisone.

4. Suspect seronegative spondyloarthropathy:

- ► If no contraindication, give full dose NSAID for 2-3 weeks and reevaluate.
- ► Corticosteroids:
  - ⇉ **Particularly useful** in complicated medical patient with underlying renal, hepatic and/or cardiac disease.
  - ⇉ Intra-articular, very useful in treatment of monoarticular acute attacks.
  - ⇉ Systemic: Consider only in patients with severe disease and in whom NSAIDs contraindicated.

REFERENCES

See standard references listed in introduction

[2] Approach to Polyarthritis/Polyarthralgia

Dr. Lori Albert, University of Toronto

KEY CONCEPTS

The diagnosis of a polyarticular condition is often a process that develops over time. There are some important features of the history and physical examination that can help to narrow the differential diagnosis, and occasionally be diagnostic. The process of developing a differential includes the following key concepts:

1. Decide if the process is articular or non-articular
2. If articular, decide if the process is inflammatory or non-inflammatory
3. Use clues from the history and physical to narrow the differential diagnosis (acuity, age, gender, joint distribution and symmetry). The presence of extra-articular manifestations is particularly helpful.
4. Laboratory data may be supportive, but generally cannot be used to establish the diagnosis
5. Follow the patient over time to firmly establish the diagnosis and refine therapy

HISTORY

Patient Demographics

Young men: Think viral and other infectious causes, reactive, psoriatic or enteropathic, sarcoid

Young women: Think viral/infectious, SLE and RA

Older men: Think polyarticular gout (usually past history of gout). Consider RA, PsA with appropriate history, OA

Older women: RA still likely. Also consider polyarticular gout with involvement of smaller joints of the fingers in elderly women as well as CPPD, OA

Key Questions

In order to narrow down your diagnosis, you want to decide if it is:

- ► Acute or chronic
- ► Truly an articular process or non-articular (or periarticular)
- ► Inflammatory or noninflammatory
- ► Determine the pattern of onset and pattern of involvement
- ► Is there axial (spinal) involvement
- ► Look for helpful extra-articular features

1. How long have you had this problem?

- ► Less than 6 weeks may be infectious (usually viral) but can also be first presentation of a chronic arthropathy

2. Is there pain through the whole range of motion of an involved joint (articular) or only with movement in certain directions (non-articular)?

- ► Point to the location of the pain- true articular pain may be referred to another site (shoulder pain felt in upper arm, hip pain felt in groin)

3. Are there inflammatory features?

- ► Joint swelling (vs generalized soft tissue swelling)?
- ► Erythema-implies more intense inflammation seen only with infectious or crystal arthritis. If redness seen in RA, consider secondary infection.
- ► Prolonged **morning stiffness** (> 30min-1 hr implies inflammatory process)
- ► Decreased range of motion of affected joints

4. How did it come on?

Gradual and insidious onset:
- ▶ typical for early onset of inflammatory arthritis such as RA or Psoriatic Arthritis

Acute onset:
- ▶ Typical for viral arthritis
- ▶ Typical for reactive arthritis with history of time lag after a precipitating GI or GU infection can be seen with RA but less common (sometimes explosive onset)

Pattern of Progression	Disease
Migratory - symptoms present in some joints for a few days, then remit, but new joints become involved	Infectious (neisseria, rheumatic fever)
Additive - symptoms present in some joints and persist, and then new joints become involved and persist	Seropositive, some seronegative
Intermittent - attacks of multiple joint involvement with complete resolution in between attacks	Crystal induced (polyarticular gout), early RA, early psoriatic, reactive, sarcoid arthritis

5. What Joints are involved?

The presence of axial involvement puts patient into seronegative category since rheumatoid arthritis and other seropositive diseases do not have spine involvement (except for C-spine in RA).

Presence of inflammatory back involvement characterized by:
- ▶ Insidious onset
- ▶ Low back/buttock pain
- ▶ Prolonged morning stiffness
- ▶ Pain relieved by moving around

Seronegative arthritis tends to be:
- ▶ Asymmetrical
- ▶ Lower extremity predominates
- ▶ Larger joints (knees, ankles, hips)

▶ Enthesitis (inflammation of insertion of tendon and ligament into bone)
  ▸ Achilles, plantar fasciitis common (causes of "heel pain")
▶ Dactylitis (inflammation of tendon sheath producing "sausage digit")
  ▸ Think Psoriatic Arthritis or Reactive Arthritis

Seropositive arthritis tends to be:
  ▶ Symmetrical
  ▶ Small and large joints
    ▸ MCP/PIP involvment with sparing of DIP's in RA
    ▸ MTP involvement common
    ▸ PIP involvement in SLE
    ▸ DIP spared in seropositive diseases
  ▶ Upper and lower extremity evenly affected

6. Do you have any symptoms outside of the joints (ie. Extra-articular features)

Easiest to divide these according to "seropositive" and "seronegative"

Systemic: Fever, fatigue, weight loss may suggest more significant inflammatory disease

	Diseases	Extra-Articular Features (EAF's)
Seropositive	RA, SLE, other connective tissue diseases	Facial rash, other rash, photosensitivity, oral ulcers, alopecia, Raynaud's, sicca, serositis, nodules
Seronegative	Reactive, psoriatic, enteropathic, ankylosing spondylitis, undifferentiated seronegative disease	Oral ulcers, conjunctivitis, uveitis, GU symptoms, GI symptoms, psoriatic rash, keratoderma blenorrhagicum, balanitis, enthesitis (inflammation at insertion of ligaments and tendons into bone), dactylitis (sausage digit)

Other important information from history:

Other medical illnesses

- ► Inflammatory bowel disease (think enteropathic arthritis)
- ► Psoriasis (think psoriatic arthritis)
- ► Iritis/uveitis (think seronegative, HLAB27 associated diseases)
  - ⇥ Other eye involvement can be seen in RA
- ► Thyroid, diabetes, etc. can be associated with msk complaints
- ► Recent symptoms of infection, particularly
  - ⇥ GU (think Reactive Arthritis)
  - ⇥ GI (think Reactive Arthritis)
  - ⇥ Sore throat (think rheumatic fever, viral, SLE (non-infectious))

Family history

- ► Seronegative arthritis, psoriasis, IBD
- ► RA or SLE
- ► Osteoarthritis

Medications

- ► Informative to learn what medications have been tried that help msk symptoms (eg. anti-inflammatories)
- ► Medications used for other reasons, especially new ones, may give clues to iatrogenic disease eg. drug induced lupus, serum sickness reaction to penicillins, gout exacerbated by diuretic use, etc.

Functional Capacity

How has your life been affected by this problem?

1. Personal care - dressing, bathing, grooming, toileting
2. Daily activities - cooking, cleaning, shopping
3. Driving
4. Work and hobbies
5. Exercise, walking

Previous Investigations

- ► What if any bloodwork/imaging studies have been done that might give clues?

PHYSICAL EXAMINATION

Vitals: Look for tachycardia , tachypnea, fever, hypertension (signs that there is some systemic process or involvement of organs other than the joints)

Head and Neck: alopecia, ocular inflammation, oral and nasal ulcerations, nasal discharge or bleeding (Vasculitis- Wegener's specifically), malar rash, telangectasia, lymphadenopathy, thyroid

Chest: tachypnea, crackles (interstitial lung involvement associated with some rheumatic diseases), pleural effusions (SLE or RA), chest expansion as part of spine exam

CVS: murmurs (think RF), rubs (SLE, RA), loss of pulses, asymmetrical BP, bruits (think large vessel vasculitis)

Skin and nails: psoriasis, other rashes (think SLE), periungual erythema (think SLE and other connective tissue diseases), livedo reticularis (think SLE with anti-phospholipid antibody syndrome, or vasculitis), nodules (think RA), ulcerations (think scleroderma, vasculitis), erythema nodosum (think enteropathic arthritis, sarcoid), telangiectasia(think CREST, scleroderma)

Neurologic: neuropathy (vasculitis), carpal tunnel syndrome, CNS abnormalities (SLE)

MSK:
Determine that joints are inflammatory vs noninflammatory
- ▶ Active or inflamed joints characterized on examination by joint line tenderness or stress pain, warmth, erythema, effusion, decreased range of motion

Look for additional sites of joint involvement of which patient may be unaware. Assess for spine involvement
- ▶ **Schober test:** 10cm distance marked above midpoint between the posterior superior iliac spines increases to 15cm with forward flexion in normal spine.
- ▶ **Measure finger-to-fibula distance** with lateral flexion, and **finger-to-floor** distance with forward flexion as ways of monitoring spine

involvement
- ▶ **Chest expansion:** normal 4-6cm with tape measure around nipple line from *end-expiration to end-inspiration*
- ▶ **Occiput-to-wall distance:** should be 0cm with back against wall, heels touching wall

Look at distribution of peripheral joints: "Pattern Recognition"

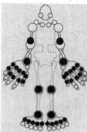

Symmetrical Large
and small joints
- ▶ Seropositive diseases
- ▶ PsA (may have DIP
  involvement as well)

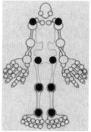

Symmetrical Large
joint polyarthritis
- ▶ Seronegative
  arthropathy (often
  with spondylitis)
- ▶ Rheumatoid Arthritis

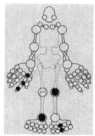

Asymmetrical Oligo-
or polyarthritis
- ▶ Seronegative
- ▶ Crystal-induced
- ▶ Infectious

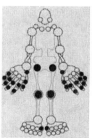

Symmetrical large
and small joint,
non-inflammatory:
- ▶ OA (note DIP
  involvement)

KEY LABORATORY INVESTIGATIONS

CBC: look for anemia and thrombocytosis as signs of inflammation, cytopenias as part of a lupus picture, lymphopenia secondary to viral infection or SLE

ESR: not specific, but may support a more systemic inflammatory process

Creatinine, urinalysis: screening prior to therapy, look for signs of GN (SLE,vasculitis)

LFT: screening prior to therapy , look for signs of hepatitis related process

Special: Consider RF, ANA, C3,C4, ANCA if clinical picture is suggestive (review chapter on laboratory tests for other causes of positive ANA and RF)

Serum urate: if clinical picture is suggestive of gout (not helpful in setting of acute inflammation)

IMAGING

Plain radiographs: unlikely to be helpful with acute process (unlikely to see radiographic changes within joints such as erosions, osteophytes etc.)
In early stages may appreciate soft tissue swelling, peri-articular osteopenia

With more longstanding process
- ▶ Consider Xrays of hands and feet (can pick up early erosions in MTP joints)
- ▶ Consider Xrays of SI joints and lumbar spine if seronegative disease is suspected

CT and MRI: unlikely to be useful in polyarticular disease

Technetium bone Scan: Consider if difficulty in establishing diagnosis (articular vs nonarticular)

Gallium Scan: rarely useful in polyarticular process as bacterial infection of multiple joints simultaneously would be very unusual

DIFFERENTIAL DIAGNOSES

Causes of Acute (< 6 weeks) Inflammatory Polyarthritis	
Infectious	*Non-infectious*
Viral (rubella, hepatitis B&C, parvovirus, EBV, HIV Bacterial (gonococcal,meningococcal) Bacterial endocarditis Lyme disease Acute rheumatic fever	Rheumatoid arthritis (new onset) Reactive arthritis SLE Psoriatic arthritis Polyarticular gout Serum sickness Juvenile rheumatoid arthritis Sarcoid arthritis

Causes of Chronic (> 6 weeks) Inflammatory Polyarthritis

Rheumatoid arthritis
SLE
Psoriatic arthritis
Other collagen vascular diseases
Reactive arthritis
Enteropathic arthritis or other seronegative arthropathy
Polyarticular gout
CPPD
Juvenile rheumatoid arthritis/Still's disease
Vasculitis
Sarcoid arthritis

Causes of Non-inflammatory Polyarticular Symptoms

Osteoarthritis
CPPD
Polyarticular gout
Others: Hemachromatosis, ochronosis, acromegaly,
benign hypermobility syndrome

Non-articular Causes of Polyarticular Symptoms
Polymyalgia rheumatica (primarily proximal pain and stiffness) Fibromyalgia (pain, fatigue and sleep disturbance) Polymyositis (primarily weakness, occasionally pain)

INITIAL THERAPY

NON-PHARMACOLOGIC

Although every new patient with inflammatory polyarthritis may not need to see or have the benefit of seeing allied health staff, treatment must include basic principles from these disciplines.

Occupational Therapy

- ► Rest the affected joints
    - ➤ Splints can be very effective for hand and wrist involvement
    - ➤ Bed rest may be needed for extensive joint involvement

- ► Energy conservation (use periods of rest to maintain function)
- ► Use of adaptive/assistive devices to minimize work of involved joints

Physical Therapy

- ► Ice acutely inflamed joints
- ► Heat (eg. hot wax) may be good for more chronically inflamed joints or OA
- ► Gentle exercise needed early to prevent loss of function

Patient education is very important to adherence to investigations and therapy.

PHARMACOLOGIC

NSAIDs

- ► Avoid if any suggestion of renal involvement/hepatic involvement or history of peptic ulcer disease
- ► Mainstay of initial management in most cases
- ► NSAID choice depends on physician/patient preference, cost, availability, etc. Ensure therapeutic dose, monitor creatinine and liver enzymes. Protection against GI complications (e.g. misoprostol, PPI) in high risk patient (see therapeutics chapter).

Corticosteroids

- ▶ Appropriate for systemic rheumatic disease where diagnosis has been made or investigations are pending, infection has been ruled out and NSAIDs are contra-indicated or ineffective. Use lowest dose
- ▶ Sample doses:
  - ▸ Polyarticular gout: Prednisone 25-30mg/d x several days then taper
  - ▸ SLE: Prednisone 10-20 mg/d in absence of other significant systemic disease. Prednisone 0.5- 1 mg/kg/d (if internal organ involvement)
  - ▸ Systemic vasculitis: Prednisone 1 mg/kg/d (with internal organ involvement)
  - ▸ Rheumatoid arthritis: AVOID use UNLESS needed as bridge while waiting for DMARDS to work or DMARDs incompletely effective. Use prednisone 10mg/d or less
  - ▸ Route of administration: oral single or divided dosing usually acceptable
  - ▸ IV equivalents can be used in severely ill patients

Intra-articular Corticosteroids

For individual, severely affected joints- ensure infection is ruled out.

DMARDS (Disease Modifying Anti-Rheumatic Drugs/immunosuppressive agents) are often required early (eg. rheumatoid arthritis, systemic vasculitis) but generally consultation with rheumatologist recommended if these drugs are to be used (see therapeutics chapter).

REFERENCES

See standard references listed in introduction
Klinkhoff, A. Can. Med. Assoc. Journal 2000; 162(13), 1833-38.
Ensworth,S. Can. Med. Assoc. Journal 2000; 163(7), 1011-16.

[3] Approach to the Patient Who "Hurts All Over"

Dr. Heather McDonald-Blumer,
University of Toronto

KEY CONCEPTS

When a patient presents to the Emergency Department or is seen on the ward with widespread musculoskeletal pain, the differential diagnosis is considerable. The differential may include musculoskeletal causes as well as possible neurologic processes although the latter is beyond the scope of this summary. Generally, widespread MSK pain is considered to be present when the patient complains of pain above and below the waist and usually involving the left and right sides of the body. In the Emergency Department, the key is to determine whether or not the diffuse pain has a benign cause or is of a more worrisome etiology. Meticulous attention to the history is important to gather the appropriate information. The physical examination is often less helpful in distinguishing one type of process from another but laboratory tests can be useful adjuncts.

The focus of this section will be on Fibromyalgia Syndrome (FMS) as it is the most common rheumatologic cause of chronic, diffuse MSK pain. Remember, this is a description of a patient's complaints, not a diagnosis. It is important to consider and rule out other pathology when trying to establish a label of fibromyalgia.

The current criteria for the classification of FMS include:

- ► History of widespread pain
  - ⇥ Bilateral
  - ⇥ Above and below the waist
  - ⇥ Axial distribution
- ► Pain in 11 of 18 "tender points"

FMS can occur in isolation and thus be the sole cause of musculoskeletal symptoms. However, it can occur in conjunction with other disease processes, again emphasizing the need for a detailed clinical assessment.

PATIENT DEMOGRAPHICS

Chronic, widespread MSK pain is common and has been estimated to have a prevalence of 2% of the adult population in Canada. Adults of any age can present with widespread musculoskeletal pain. In the elderly, especially those over age 65, consideration must be given to processes such as polymyalgia rheumatica (PMR) with or without associated temporal arteritis (TA). In any age group, diffuse MSK pain may be part of a process such as Rheumatoid Arthritis or even, other systemic connective tissue diseases. Muscle pain plus weakness suggests processes such as inflammatory myopathies. In female patients, in early and mid adulthood, thought must be given to the process of fibromyalgia which is seen predominantly, although not exclusively, in women. Less commonly, and in no particular relation to age or gender, metabolic, infectious or paraneoplastic processes must also be considered. Travel history is important in this group.

HISTORY OF PRESENTING ILLESS
The key questions:

1. What regions are involved?

- ▶ The common complaint on history from a FMS pt is
  - ⟫ "Total body pain"
  - ⟫ "I hurt all over"
- ▶ on direct questioning neck and shoulder girdle, lower back and hip girdle pain are common (above and below the waist, bilateral)
- ▶ to distinguish from PMR - age over 65, sudden onset, prolonged morning stiffness and supporting lab work can be helpful
- ▶ no identifiable precipitant
- ▶ the clinical features of Temporal Arteritis must also be evaluated (see section on vasculitis)
- ▶ to distinguish from myopathies - proximal muscle weakness occurs in myopathies but true weakness doesn't occur in FMS - the presence of pain in the muscle groups may give the patient the perception of weakness which make this difficult to distinguish from history alone

2. How did it come on?

- ▶ gradual and insidious is the most common pattern in FMS however, trauma such as an MVA is also common with the acute pain from a whiplash type injury never appearing to settle and gradually becoming more generalized

▶ this can be contrasted with the usually acute onset of pain in PMR; sub-acute onset can be seen in all but probably most common in myopathies

3. Does the patient have morning stiffness?

▶ not very helpful as many of the causes of widespread MSK pain can be associated with prolonged morning stiffness

▶ In an elderly patient with PMR, recent onset of stiffness is typical. In FMS, it is not unusual for patients to have several hours of morning stiffness, although joint range of movement is usually normal (that is, they can make a grip - it just feels tight and sore)

4. What are the aggravating and alleviating factors?

▶ FMS pain can fluctuate daily but is typically worse with:
  ▸ physical activity (even normal ADL)
  ▸ poor sleep
  ▸ emotional stress
  ▸ weather change

▶ If FMS is occurring concomitantly with another connective tissue disease such as RA, a flare of the inflammatory disease can aggravate FMS features

5. Is there true muscle weakness?

▶ This can be difficult to determine in some instances, as the patient may be unable to exert maximal force due to the presence of pain in the muscle groups being tested but...
  ▸ there is no true weakness in FMS
  ▸ there is no muscle weakness in PMR
  ▸ there is proximal muscle weakness in the myopathies

▶ FMS pts will complain of weakness but frequently have normal muscle strength on testing or inconsistent findings of weakness

6. Has there been a specific precipitant?

▶ if no, this fits with PMR

- ▶ a prodrome of viral like symptoms may occur prior to an infectious process (myalgias) but would be rare in inflammatory myopathies and metabolic processes

- ▶ new medications or dose alterations? e.g. Statins can cause myalgias, muscle weakness and elevated CK

- ▶ less commonly, changes in thyroid medication or new onset of clinically apparent thyroid disease

7. Are there associated findings on systems review?

- ▶ Fibromyalgia usually has no associated fever, chills, and/or sweats and weight loss is exceedingly uncommon. A patient may complain of extreme fatigue and on questioning, a non-restorative sleep pattern can be elicited. Other common findings on history include symptoms of:

  - ➠ Fatigue
  - ➠ Headaches ("migraine" or tension headaches) NB to distinguish this from the headaches of temporal arteritis
  - ➠ Irritable bowel
  - ➠ "Swollen Hands" (perceived by the patient but not clinically apparent)
  - ➠ Raynaud's phenomenon (without digital infarction or ulceration)

- ▶ Finding on history of fever, sweats and/or weight loss should make one think of other processes including:

  - ➠ Vasculitis including PMR/TA
  - ➠ myopathies
  - ➠ malignancy
  - ➠ infectious processes

- ▶ The reported level of disability can be striking and may be out of proportion to what one might expect from observing the patient during the clinical encounter (see below).

8. Have there been previous investigations?

As FMS is rarely an acute process, many FMS patients will have been investigated previously. Test results are usually normal.

9. Have previous treatments been undertaken?

In FMS, it is common for patients to have tried many analgesic (including narcotic analgesics) and anti-inflammatory medications and report minimal if any benefit.

PAST MEDICAL HISTORY

In fibromyalgia, there is often a background history of:

- ▶ Trauma - e.g. motor vehicle collisions (may be remote in time)
- ▶ Depression
- ▶ Concomitant MSK diseases such as Rheumatoid arthritis, SLE etc

Processes such as PMR/TA are not associated with any specific antecedent or pre-existing illnesses.

FAMILY MEDICAL HISTORY

Generally, this is not contributory. There is some evidence to suggest that FMS has a familial tendency. Whether this is genetic or situational is yet to be determined.

PHYSICAL EXAM

The general physical examination in patients with FMS is essentially normal. The joint exam is often normal as well in isolated FMS but note should be made that many patients with other rheumatologic diseases may also have fibromyalgia.

a. Vitals

- ▶ most often, within normal limits

b. Skin and Nails

- ▶ FMS - usually normal although dermatographism has been noted
- ▶ must observe for and rule out rashes which may suggest other illnesses such as:
    - ⇾ erythematous rash in viral illnesses
    - ⇾ Gottren's plaques in DM
    - ⇾ vasculitic lesions
    - ⇾ cutaneous finding associated with Raynaud's phenomenon

c. Head and Neck

- ▶ usually normal except for MSK findings (see below)

- ► check temporal arteries for:
    - ▸ tenderness
    - ▸ pulsation
    - ▸ thickening

temporal arteritis

- ► check visual fields
- ► check lymph nodes - consider viral or other infectious etiology
- ► assess thyroid

d. Chest

- ► normal in FMS
- ► this should include assessment of chest expansion to rule out process such as the inflammatory spondyloarthropathies. Note that inflammatory myopathies can have restrictive lung findings as well as parenchymal disease

e. CVS

- ► normal in FMS unless unrelated cardiac disease is present
- ► large vessel vasculitis can affect the aorta - therefore check for equal BP bilaterally, new heart murmurs suggesting aortic valve insufficiency, bruits

f. Abdomen

- ► should be within normal limits

g. Neurologic

- ► should be within normal limits

h. Musculoskeletal

- ► joints will usually be normal
- ► muscle tone - normal
- ► muscle bulk
    - ▸ normal in PMR, FMS, any acute process
    - ▸ may be decreased in sub-acute and chronic process - usually consistent with inflammatory and metabolic etiologies
    - ▸ significantly diminished in thyroid related myopathies
- ► muscle strength - true myopathies are associated with weakness but remember that PMR and FMS are associated with normal strength

Tender points: 18 potential tender points in total (9 bilateral pairs)

- ▶ Occipital
    - ➤ suboccipital muscle insertions
- ▶ Trapezius
    - ➤ midpoint of the upper border
- ▶ Low Cervical
    - ➤ C5-C7 transverse processes
- ▶ 2nd costochondral junction
- ▶ Lateral epicondyle
    - ➤ 2 cm distal to the epicondyle
- ▶ Supraspinatus
    - ➤ medial to the superior border of the scapula
- ▶ Gluteal
    - ➤ upper, outer quadrant of the buttock
- ▶ Lateral Trochanter
    - ➤ posterior to greater trochanteric prominence
- ▶ Medial Fat pad of the Knee
    - ➤ just proximal to the medial joint line

Increased tenderness in these areas suggest regions of hyperalgesia related to referred pain from the spine.

11/18 tender points being positive is considered "diagnostic".

DIFFERENTIAL DIAGNOSIS

Fibromyalgia is a diagnosis of exclusion. Other possible processes which need to be ruled out include:

Viral Myositis

- ▶ Influenza: myalgias are common
    - ➤ Post-influenza myositis causes severe pain in the calf or occasionally in the thigh as well as elevated CK

- ▶ Enteroviruses:
    - ➤ Coxxackie B viruses (sep B5 and B6)

- ▶ Other viral causes:
    - ➤ hepatitis B, rubella, herpes virus and RSV, HIV

Drug Induced Myopathies/Myositis

Statins
- ▶ hydroxyl-methylglutaryl-CoA (HMG-CoA) reductase inhibitors

- ▶ Simvastatin appears more likely than pravastatin
- ▶ 6-14% of patients experience myalgias
- ▶ < 1% develop myositis or rhabdomyolysis
- ▶ risk of myositis is increased in patients with:
  - ➠ low levels of cytochrome P-450 3A4
  - ➠ other medication that inhibit statin metabolism (eg. Itraconazole, cyclosporine, erythromycin)
  - ➠ electrolyte disturbances
  - ➠ infection
  - ➠ trauma
  - ➠ hypoxia

Aminoquinolones

Steroids

Penicillamiine

Colchicine

Endocrine Causes

- ▶ Hypothyroidism
- ▶ Hyperparathyroidism
- ▶ Cushing's syndrome

Para-neoplastic phenomenon

Other Rheumatologic Processes

- ▶ Inflammatory Polyarthritis
- ▶ Spondyloarthropathies

INVESTIGATIONS

Screening Laboratory Testing

CBC

- ▶ Haemoglobin
  - ➠ normal in FMS
  - ➠ decreased in many chronic rheumatologic diseases such as vasculitis, PMR/TA and the myopathies (this is usually an anaemia of chronic disease)
- ▶ Platelets
  - ➠ normal in FMS

> ⤻ Can be elevated in inflammatory processes as it is an acute phase reactant

▶ WBC - no usual change in widespread MSK pain but if abnormal, widen the differential

ESR

▶ Normal in FMS
▶ Increased (often markedly) in other inflammatory/vasculitic processes

Routine Chemistry

This will all be normal in Fibromyalgia unless other unrelated co-morbidities exist. Consider assessing the following:

▶ Creatinine - if elevated - think age, systemic vasculitis, connective tissue disease
  > ⤻ Usually normal in PMR/TA,
  > ⤻ Always normal in FMS (unless other causes)

▶ AST and ALT- can be increased in muscle injury
▶ CK - often increased in muscle injury (myopathy, myositis)
▶ TSH - rule out a thyroid myopathy

Specific Laboratory Testing

Autoimmune Serology
▶ ANA positive - can be seen in the FMS population. In the absence of other features supporting the diagnosis of a Connective Tissue Disease, these patients can still be found to have FMS

▶ ANA, anti- ds DNA, anti ENA (specifically looking at anti Jo-1, although others such as Mi-2 and PM-Sc are discussed in the literature but are often not available in usual clinical practice)

▶ Complement

Myoglobinuria

HIV, HCV, HBV

Imaging

Routine radiography
▶ often not helpful as pain is frequently muscle based, not articular
▶ In patients with dermatomyositis, there is a potential association

with malignancy and as such, further investigations may be ordered to this out (eg. CXR, mammogram etc)

MRI

▶ helpful in diagnosis of inflammatory myositis - especially in guiding location of muscle biopsy

Electromyography

Despite subjective complaints of numbness and or tingling in the hands in many patients with FMS, nerve conduction testing should be normal in this population. EMG testing would be important to pursue if considering a myopathic process.

Biopsy

▶ Tissue samples are not required and not diagnostic in FMS.
▶ Temporal Arteritis
   ▸ If you consider this as a significant possibility in your differential diagnosis - you MUST arrange for a prompt temporal biopsy

▶ Inflammatory Myopathy
   ▸ Tissue diagnosis is needed to confirm the diagnosis and assess the activity of the process and the amount of damage in the muscle fibers

TREATMENT

Non-Pharmacologic

Fibromyalgia

Organizing treatment is an ambulatory care activity. Multidisciplinary care is ideal but is very difficult to arrange and even harder for many of these patients to afford. Education and active participation are the keys, rather than prolonged attendance at a specific program.

▶ Physiotherapy/Exercise
   ▸ aerobic activities for fitness
   ▸ muscle stretching and strengthening exercises
   ▸ posture correction - proper back posture with sitting, standing and sleeping is often a helpful adjunct

▶ Physical Modalities

　　▸▸ Heat is generally beneficial and cold poorly tolerated.
　　▸▸ Physical aids such as Obus forms, orthopaedic neck pillows etc can be very useful

▶ Sleep Hygiene: Instructing and encouraging patients to pay close attention to habits which can optimize their sleep

　　▸▸ No caffeine
　　▸▸ Regular bed time
　　▸▸ Wind down time before attempting to sleep
　　▸▸ Proper night-time positioning, etc

▶ Social work support or other suitable counselling if situational stress or depression appear to be factors.

▶ Occupational therapy consultation for ADL - either at home or for the workplace

▶ Pool therapy

▶ Support groups - patients can contact the Arthritis Society

Pharmacologic

▶ Non narcotic analgesic medication: This is always appropriate to try although the pain of FMS is often refractory to non-narcotic analgesics as well as NSAID's. It is important to monitor for overuse.

▶ Narcotic Analgesics: Use of medication such as Tylenol No. 3 is not uncommon and typically, patients complain that these medications do not help their pain. The use of all narcotic analgesics should be actively discouraged in the FMS population due to lack of effectiveness and potential for inappropriate use (overuse).

▶ Tri-cyclic anti-depressants: The use of low dose TCA medications such as amitriptyline have been shown to be helpful in some patients for optimizing sleep patterns and minimizing pain. (Eg. Amitriptyline 10-50 mg po qhs).

▶ Cyclobenzaprine: This has been shown helpful especially with acute flares and for short-term use only.

▶ SSRI's: There is limited literature suggesting possible benefit of this class of medication in the FMS population but risks must be weighed carefully especially given recent concerns about the potential role of these medications in exacerbation of suicide rates. Detailed knowledge of the patient is needed along with the ability to follow the individual over the short and long term.

▶ Trigger Point Injections: There is little data to suggest any long term benefit to this approach although some practitioners use trigger point injections with lidocaine (or an equivalent) and occasionally with corticosteroid preparations in the FMS population.

SUMMARY

1. FMS is a description of pain symptoms and tender points and does not imply a specific or defined cause.

2. Patients who complain that they "hurt all over" and yet look well and have few if any findings on clinical examination along with normal lab work often have fibromyalgia.

3. It is important to rule other causes of MSK pain when you see a patient with a potential diagnosis of FMS.

4. Treatment of FMS is challenging and requires patience. Treatment must address chronicity of condition and focus on non-pharmacologic modalities. Patients should be encouraged to take responsibility for playing an active role in their own recovery.

[4] Approach to Muscle Weakness
Dr. Sharon LeClercq, University of Calgary

KEY CONCEPTS

1. Weakness may reflect neuromuscular disease in which case there is often an objective pattern of true motor impairment.

   ▶ These patients often describe specific tasks such as getting off a chair or taking objects off a top shelf that cannot be performed

   ▶ You must include pathology all the way from muscle to neuromuscular junction to peripheral nerve to spinal cord to central motor areas in your thinking

2. Weakness may be a functional complaint in which case there is no evidence of true muscle weakness

   ▶ These patients complain of feeling weak and often fatigued or played out but often do target a specific activity that cannot be performed

3. A thorough history and physical examination will distinguish between these two.

4. The distribution of muscle weakness is a helpful clue

   ▶ Generalized versus localized
   ▶ If localized, symmetric or asymmetric [regional neurologic disorder]
   ▶ If localized and symmetric is it distal [ie motor neuron disease], proximal [ie polymyositis] or specific [ie some form of muscular dystrophy]

5. Proximal muscle weakness of the shoulder and pelvic girdle is usually due to a myopathy.

6. Inflammatory myositis ie DM/PM are the most common rheumatologic disorders associated with usually painless proximal muscle weakness.

7. Muscle weakness associated with muscle pain is rare and may indicate an underlying vasculitis.

8. Muscle pain and weakness associated with exercise usually has a vascular origin such as vasculitis or a rare disorder of muscle metabolism.

9. Acute and severe generalized muscle weakness may reflect rhabdomyolysis and constitutes a medical emergency.

10. The presence of neurologic symptoms other than weakness also helps target the origin of the weakness

   ► Distal symmetric or asymmetric muscle weakness associated with neurologic symptoms such as paresthesia is more likely to reflect a neurologic lesion such as a peripheral neuropathy or a compression neuropathy.

11. Weakness and exercise induced fatigue of muscle, particularly involving the eye and bulbar muscles along with limb musculature should target the neuromuscular junction ie Myasthenia Gravis

12. Acute distal ascending weakness with loss of reflexes often following an upper respiratory illness may reflect Guillian-Barre syndrome, an acute inflammatory demyelinating polyneuropathy.

13. Severe weakness, even quadriplegia, in the face of multisystem failure in an ICU patient may reflect a combination of acute myopathy, neuromuscular blockade, peripheral nerve dysfunction and drug induced weakness.

14. A mixed picture with muscle weakness, atrophy and muscle fasciculation combined with upper motor neuron signs may reflect motor neuron disease [Lou Gehrig's disease].

15. Rarely, weakness with a background of poliomyelitis may present in adult life with progressive weakness, fatigue and muscle pain.

HISTORY

Specific questions to ask about "weakness"

   ► What does the patient mean by "weakness"?
   ► Can they give an example of an activity limitation ie getting off the toilet?
   ► What is the distribution of muscle involvement: large muscles [getting up to walk] or small muscles [grasping and holding on to objects] or both?
   ► How fast has the weakness progressed?
   ► How have the symptoms changed since onset?
   ► Has there been a slow or intermittent decline in strength?

- ▶ Are there any difficulties with vision, speech or swallowing?
- ▶ Is there any pattern to the weakness such as worse after exercise?
- ▶ Does the weakness worsen with repetitive action?
- ▶ Are there any associated central or peripheral neurologic symptoms such as paresthesia, bladder or bowel control problems, incoordination
- ▶ Has there been any trouble with skin rash?
- ▶ Has there been any general disturbance such as fever, night sweats or weight loss?
- ▶ Has there been a recent weight gain associated with cold intolerance and dry skin/hair
- ▶ Has there been any recent severe illness?
- ▶ Have they started any new medications in the last 6 months?

After asking these questions, you should have an idea if the patient's complaints are due an intrinsic problem with the neuromuscular system or if it may be a reflection of a general systemic illness.

Past medical problems

- ▶ Any history of chronic disease such as heart, lung or kidney?
- ▶ Any history of chronic infections?
- ▶ Any past history of childhood illness such as poliomyelitis?

Medications

- ▶ Review the general list of drugs
- ▶ Any known drugs to cause muscle problems such as statins?
- ▶ Are they taking any medications that might cause secondary effects on muscle such as a diuretic which may lower serum K to a level that influences muscle function?
- ▶ Are they taking any over the counter medications or naturopathic medications?

Family history

- ▶ Any history of autoimmune disease?
- ▶ Any history of endocrine diseases such as hypothyroidism?
- ▶ Any history of inherited disorders - muscle or neurologic?

Social and Personal

- ▶ Any history past or present of depression?
- ▶ Any stress related problems ?
- ▶ Drugs and IV exposure? Hep B or C?

▶ Sexual history ?HIV

Systems review

In a patient with functional weakness, the systems review may need to be extensive to cover the possibilities outlined below. In these individuals, weakness has to be separated from fatigue, poor endurance, weakness due to pain when attempting to perform an activity,

Underlying problems that may contribute to "weakness":

Anemia	Deconditioning
Arthritis	Depression
Cardiac disease	Endocrinopathies
Chronic infection ie HIV	Malignancy
Chronic inflammatory disease	Metabolic disease
Chronic lung disease	Renal diseases

PHYSICAL EXAMINATION

General appearance:

▶ Looks well or unwell ie SOB, cyanotic, pale
▶ Able or not able to rise from the chair to walk across the room
▶ Gower's sign = patient attempts to rise from a chair by climbing up legs with his hands

Vital signs:

▶ Expected to be normal in most inflammatory myositis patients; otherwise may reflect underlying disease

Skin and nails:

▶ Findings in Dermatomyositis:
▶ Heliotrope = a violaceous rash on the upper eyelids accompanied by swelling
▶ Erythema in a shawl or V region of upper chest and back
▶ Gottron's sign = symmetrical nonscaling violaceous erythematous rash over the extensor surface of MCP and PIP areas of fingers
▶ Periungual erythema due to nailfold abnormalities [vessel dropout/dilated loops]
▶ Subcutaneous calcification
▶ Butterfly rash of SLE
▶ Tethered thin skin of Scleroderma in the hands
▶ Telangiectasia of CREST syndrome

Head and neck:
- ▶ Thyroid enlargement
- ▶ Parotid or salivary gland enlargement
- ▶ Adenopathy
- ▶ Weakness of the tongue or oropharynx
- ▶ Dry mouth and excessive caries in keeping with Sjogren's

Pulmonary:
- ▶ Look for evidence of restrictive lung disease, parenchymal disease or pleural disease

Cardiovascular:
- ▶ Look for evidence of heart failure (especially tachycardia early on), valvular disease
- ▶ Are all pulses present? Any bruits?

Abdominal:
- ▶ Look for masses, organomegaly, bruits

Renal:
- ▶ Flank pain
- ▶ Peripheral edema

Neurologic:
- ▶ Optic nerve changes i.e. pallor due to MS
- ▶ Cranial nerve findings ie ptosis due to Myasthenia Gravis
- ▶ Muscle wasting and distribution ie pattern of muscular dystrophy?
- ▶ Muscle power: see Table 1 for testing/grading muscle power
- ▶ Specific groups to assess:
    - ▸ Neck flexors
    - ▸ Shoulder abduction
    - ▸ Grip strength
    - ▸ Truncal power - partial sit up ie raise the shoulders off the table
    - ▸ Rise from a squat or the chair
    - ▸ Heel and toe walk
- ▶ Reflexes; normal, increased, absent or delayed
- ▶ Sensory changes: dermatomal, peripheral nerve, cord or central
- ▶ Observation of gait ie ataxic due to posterior column problems, foot drop due to L5 lesion

MSK:
- ▶ Screening joint exam - Inflammatory joint findings ?SLE, MCTD

► Mechanic's hands = painful rough hands with cracked skin on the tips and sides of the fingers ?DM

Medical Research Council Grading For Muscle Weakness	
Grade 5	normal strength
Grade 4	muscle contraction possible against gravity and some resistance
Grade 3	muscle contraction possible against gravity only
Grade 2	muscle contraction possible only with gravity removed
Grade 1	flicker of muscle contraction but no movement of extremity
Grade 0	No contraction

There is a wide range of muscle strength and +/- values are often added

At this point, it is usually clear whether or not the weakness is due to a myopathy. The most common rheumatologic disorder presenting with weakness is an inflammatory myositis such as DM/PM.

Typical Presentation of PM/DM

► In adults, peak ages of 45 - 55
► Ratio of women to men is 2-3:1
► Insidious onset of painless proximal weakness over several months
► Usually neck and shoulder girdle then trunk and pelvic girdle
► Distal strength is usually not a major concern
► Erythematous rash on eyelids, sun exposed areas and extensor surfaces
► May have other complaints as well as weakness:Fatigue, weight loss, arthralgia, heartburn, dyspnea
► Elevated CK levels often in the thousands [>1000 but < 10,000]

Diagnostic Criteria for DM/PM

► Symmetric proximal muscle weakness
► Typical rash of Dermatomyositis
► Elevated serum muscle enzymes
► Myopathic changes on EMG
► Characteristic muscle biopsy abnormalities and absence of histopathologic findings of other myopathies

Classification of DM/PM

- ▶ Adult Polymyositis
- ▶ Adult Dermatomyositis
- ▶ PM/DM associated with malignancy
- ▶ Childhood DM
- ▶ DM/PM associated with other connective tissue diseases

INVESTIGATIONS

General tests:

- ▶ CBC; liver function; renal function biochemistry including electrolytes, calcium, magnesium and phosphorus; ESR; Thyroid function tests; muscle enzymes
- ▶ Muscle enzymes include CK [creatine kinase], Aldolase, LDH [lactic dehydrogenase], AST [aspartate aminotransferase]
- ▶ The CK is the most sensitive and specific for muscle disease
- ▶ The CK may rise several weeks before muscle strength changes
- ▶ The CK may also fall before clinical improvement in strength after therapy is initiated
- ▶ The CK can be useful in monitoring response to therapy

Additional tests:

- ▶ ECG and Chest Xray
- ▶ Renal/pelvic/abdominal ultrasound [? malignancy]
- ▶ Mammogram [? malignancy]
- ▶ MRI [? Malignancy or to target a site for biopsy]

Specific tests:

- ▶ EMG and nerve conduction studies
- ▶ Muscle biopsy
- ▶ +/- nerve biopsy [considering a systemic vasculitis with neurologic symptoms]
- ▶ Skin biopsy
- ▶ Autoantibodies
- ▶ Hepatitis serology
- ▶ Cryoglobulins
- ▶ Complement levels
- ▶ PTH or ACTH levels or GH [considering an endocrinopathy]

Autoantibodies:

- ▶ Antinuclear antibodies are found in up to 80% of DM/PM patients

- Several antibodies may reflect disease overlaps
  - Anti-RNP with mixed connective tissue disease [SLE, PM, Scleroderma]
  - Anti-Ku and anti-PM-Scl in Scleroderma-PM overlaps
- Myositis specific antibodies are present in up to 1/3 of patients
  - Anti-Jo1 = anti-histadyl-tRNA synthetase; strongly associated with interstitial lung disease, Raynaud's, mechanic's hands, arthritis
  - Anti-Mi-2 = anti-helicase; acute onset of classic DM, may be linked with certain epitopes on HLA molecules
  - Anti-SRP = anti-signal recognition peptide; severe drug resistant PM with cardiac involvement

Electromyography:

- Document the presence of a myopathy
- Typical findings in an inflammatory myopathy include
  - Small polyphasic action potentials
  - Fibrillations, positive sharp waves, insertional irritability
  - Repetitive high frequency action potentials
- Ascertain the presence and severity of a neuropathy

Nerve Conduction Studies:

- Localize anatomic lesions in the peripheral nerves
- A classic example is the median nerve in carpal tunnel compression
- Ascertain if there is axonal or demyelinating disease

Muscle Biopsy:

- Biopsy a clinically weak muscle but avoid EMG site
- Specimen must be appropriately handled for later testing [routine and EM, special biochemical tests]
- MRI scanning can target affected muscle
- Typical features of inflammatory myositis
  - necrosis and regeneration of muscle fibers
  - variation of fiber size
  - endomysial inflammatory cell infiltration and perivascular inflammation with CD8+ T cells in PM
  - chronic inflammatory cell infiltrate in the perivascular and perifascicular areas CD4+ T cells and B cells in DM

DIFFERENTIAL DIAGNOSIS

Polymyositis and Dermatomyositis

- ► Clinical differences
    - ⇉ DM has characteristic skin findings and is associated with higher incidence of malignancy
- ► Pathologic differences
    - ⇉ DM is associated with immune complex deposition in vessels whereas PM is due to a direct T-cell mediated attack on muscle
- ► PM may also appear as part of a chronic graft versus host reaction

Inclusion Body Myositis

- ► Most commonly confused with PM
- ► More insidious onset with slower progression
- ► Features both proximal and distal weakness
- ► Males>females
- ► Mean age of onset = 60
- ► CK values are not as high [<10x normal]
- ► Biopsy reveals inflammatory changes, but the hallmark is the presence of filamentous inclusions and vacuoles on EM
- ► Poor response to therapy

Myositis associated with other autoimmune illnesses

- ► Usually occurs along with other features of the illness
- ► Usually quite responsive to steroid therapy
- ► Occasionally is the primary problem and behaves in an aggressive fashion

Infection related myositis

- ► HIV can be associated with general debility and a specific inflammatory myopathy
- ► Other cases in which muscle is directly infected ie Trichinosis

Other inflammatory myopathies

- ► Sarcoidosis can be associated with several types of myopathy including a picture like PM and a nodular form of inflammation

Toxic myopathies

- ► Cocaine use has been associated with acute rhabdomyolysis

Drug related myopathies

- ► Colchicine can cause a myopathy, especially when used in the face of renal failure

▶ Nowadays the most common drug related myopathy is due to statin use

Endocrine related myopathies

▶ Hypothyroidism can cause a proximal myopathy with elevated levels of CK

Inherited myopathies

▶ Accompany disorders in lipid and carbohydrate metabolism and often feature post exertional muscle pain and weakness

Malignancy related myopathy

▶ When to consider this?
   ➤ Greatest risk in patients > 45 years of age presenting with DM particularly
   ➤ The malignances are those expected of the corresponding age group
   ➤ In some studies, ovarian cancer more common than expected
▶ What investigations should be done?
   ➤ Specific: target any area of patient complaint ie weight loss and abdominal pain and pursue in-depth investigations
   ➤ General: CBC and differential, urinalysis, liver function tests, stools for OB, Chest, abdominal and pelvic CT scan, mammograms

Muscular Dystrophy

Motor neuron disease

Myasthenia gravis

Rhabodomyolysis

▶ Muscle necrosis and release of toxic muscle contents such as heme pigment into circulation
▶ May cause a life threatening illness due to acute renal failure
▶ The cause is usually apparent ie crush injury or other traumas, infections, toxins including alcohol, metabolic disturbances such as hypokalemia, unusual and severe physical exercise, etc
▶ If there is no apparent cause, consider the possibility of a rare abnormality in carbohydrate or lipid metabolism. ie Carnitine palmitoyltransferase = CPT deficiency
▶ Here the clue might be recurrent attacks of muscle pain after exercise and cramps

Presentation of rhabdomyolysis

- ▶ Muscle pain +/- muscle weakness depending on the degree of damage
- ▶ Myoglobinuria and pigmenturia
- ▶ Elevated CK levels - often extremely high ie >10,000
- ▶ May present in overt renal failure with rising serum creatinine and abnormal electrolytes

Management

- ▶ Volume expansion with IV isotonic saline
- ▶ Alkaline-mannitol diuresis
- ▶ Monitoring of renal function and blood chemistry (hyperkalemia, hyperphosophatemia, hypocalcemia), consultation early to nephrology if suspicious
- ▶ Consultation early to Nephrology as soon as suspicious

TREATMENT OPTIONS

Polymyositis

- ▶ Corticosteroids with a dose of 1 - 1.5 mg per kg in divided doses until strength improves and CK normalizes; thereafter slow taper
- ▶ In severe disease or steroid resistant disease, immunosuppressive agents can be added such as Methotrexate or Azathioprine, less often Cyclosporin or Cyclophosphamide

Dermatomyositis

- ▶ Corticosteroids as above
- ▶ Immunosuppressive agents as above
- ▶ Hydroxychloroquine for cutaneous disease
- ▶ Experimental for refractory disease: IVIG, Cellcept, and TNF blockers

Inclusion body myopathy

- ▶ Poor response to therapy
- ▶ Trial of corticosteroids warranted
- ▶ Rare response to immunosuppressive agents

Monitoring response to therapy

- ▶ Follow muscle strength
- ▶ Follow CK
- ▶ Monitor for side effects from steroid
- ▶ Monitor for side effects from immunosuppressive therapy
    - ▸ ie MTX: CBC and differential every 2 weeks initially and sub-

sequently, every 4 weeks, periodic liver function and serum creatinine every 4 months

Expected responses to therapy

- ▶ Most patients respond quickly to corticosteroid
- ▶ Many patients will relapse within the first 2 years
- ▶ Up to 1/3 have chronic or persistent disease

What to do in the patient who initially responds but then begins to deteriorate?

- ▶ Could this be due to steroid myopathy or is it a disease flare?
- ▶ The CK is normal in steroid myopathy
- ▶ The EMG usually is normal or shows mild changes
- ▶ If suspected, withdraw the steroid and follow muscle strength

The treatment of myositis which is a reflection of another illness such as SLE or Vasculitis is based upon the primary illness as well as the type of muscle disease present. For instance, patients with Scleroderma have several types of muscle disease including a picture of PM which may respond to steroid as well as a low grade infiltrative process which does not require steroid therapy. Corticosteroids are usually used as well as Methotrexate or other agents such as immunosuppressive agents.

[5] Approach to Raynaud's phenomenon

Dr. Janet Pope, University of Western Ontario

KEY CONCEPTS

1. Raynaud's phenomenon (RP) is reversible vasospasm of the digits with pallor and then cyanosis and/or rubor.

   ▶ Pallor must be present

2. It is common (at least 2 % of the population with onset usually in teens if idiopathic).

3. There are two types of RP

   Primary: idiopathic - not related to other diseases

   Secondary: related to other connective tissue diseases such as SLE, Sjogren's syndrome, scleroderma, RA, polymyositis

   Those with ANA+ and superficial dilated capillaries are more likely to develop a connective tissue disease at 5 years

4. Calcium channel blockers are the main pharmacologic treatment for RP

HISTORY

Demographics

Primary RP

- ▶ Not associated with structural vascular change or ischemic tissue damage - sometimes called Raynaud's disease
- ▶ Onset often in young people
- ▶ More common onset in teens and especially <40 yrs
- ▶ 1 to 3% of population
- ▶ Female preponderance
- ▶ May be a family history and there may also be migraines

Secondary RP

- ▶ Accompanied by a connective tissue disease
- ▶ Onset at any age, but especially accounts for older onset RP
- ▶ Often more severe and can be accompanied by digital ulcers, autoamputations
- ▶ Occurs in most patients with scleroderma and 10 to 20% of Sjogren's, SLE, RA
- ▶ Still female preponderance as the connective tissue diseases are more common in women
- ▶ May have a family history and may also have migraines

Key Points

- ▶ There must be pallor of fingertips and or toes, so cyanosis alone is not RP
- ▶ RP usually accompanied by cyanosis and then rubor and pain with rewarming the digits
- ▶ Review of systems for connective tissue diseases (CTD) an essential part of assessment
- ▶ Physical exam an essential part of assessment. Look particularly for dilated nailfold capillaries which are common in secondary RP

HPI

- ▶ Age of onset, description of RP, frequency and severity of attacks
- ▶ Any secondary sequelae such as ulcers or gangrene
- ▶ ROS for CTD (oral ulcers, rash, photosensitivity, alopecia, dry eyes/mouth, gland swelling, puffy fingers, tight skin, inflammation of joints, kidney problems, serositis (pleurisy, pericarditis))
- ▶ Family history for RP and CTD
- ▶ Does it interfere with your life?
- ▶ Do you need/want medications to treat it?

PHYSICAL EXAM

Vitals: expected to be normal

Skin and nails: look for rashes, photosensitivity
*Look for superficial dilated capillaries (drop out of capillaries with dilatation and hypertrophy of remaining vessels). You can use an ophthalmoscope or otoscope and see red dots or lines at the periungual area. This is highly suggestive of secondary RP

Head and neck: Look for dry eyes, mouth, lymph and salivary, lacrimal gland swelling, oral ulcers, alopecia

Chest: Look for effusions or rubs (uncommon) looking for serosits

Abdomen: usually normal

Neurologic: usually normal

MSK: Look for inflamed joints

KEY LABORATORY TESTING

No tests are confirmatory. However, if you suspect secondary RP, check ANA*,CBC, creatinine, urinalysis.

*Those with +ANA and superficial dilated capillaries are more likely to develop a connective tissue disease (20% at 5 years, especially limited systemic scleroderma, esp if ANA is anticentromere Ab positive)

IMAGING

None useful in this setting.

DIFFERENTIAL DIAGNOSIS

Primary vs Secondary RP

- ▶ Acrocyanosis or cryoglobulinemia if blue digits but no pallor
- ▶ Cryoglobulinemia especially if lower extremities involved

Classification of Secondary RP

Vasospastic

- ▶ Primary RP
- ▶ Drug induced (eg. ergot)
- ▶ Pheochromocytoma, carcinoid

Structural

A. Large and medium vessels
Thoracic outlet syndrome
Crutches
Brachycephalic trunk disease
(e.g. Takayasu's Arthritis, atherosclerosis)

B. Small arteries and arterioles
Connective tissue disease
Vibration
Cold injury
Chemotherapy (eg. Bleomycin)
Berger's disease

Hematologic

- ▶ Cryoglobulinemia and other paraproteins
- ▶ Cold agglutinins
- ▶ Polycythemia rubra vera
- ▶ Antiphospholipid antibody syndrome

TREATMENT OPTIONS

Nonpharmacologic (unproven):

- ▶ Stay warm (avoid cold, mittens are warmer than gloves, wear a hat)
- ▶ Stop smoking, avoid stress

Pharmacologic:

- ▶ Calcium channel blockers are the mainstay of therapy if prescription medications are necessary. Often use prn in winter or with season change.
- ▶ Nifedipine (long-acting), amlodipine, felodipine.
- ▶ Others:
    - ▸ Angiotensin II blockers such as losartan
    - ▸ SSRI such as prozac
    - ▸ Betablockers with ca channel blockers may help
    - ▸ Sildenafil
    - ▸ IV prostacyclins (iloprost, PGE if severe)
    - ▸ Bosentan (endothelin-1 inhibitor) - under study

REFERENCES

1. Seibold JR. Connective tissue diseases characterized by fibrosis. In: Kelley W, Harris E, Ruddy S, Sludge C, eds. Textbook of Rheumatology. 5th ed. Philadelphia: W.B. Saunders Company; 1997. p. 1139-42.

2. Tugwell P, Pope JE, Furst D. Treatment of Secondary Raynaud's. BMJ Clinical Evidence, BMJ Publishing Group, London 2003 (in press).

3. Pope J. Raynaud's phenomenon (primary). Clinical Evidence 2003 Jun;(9):1339-1348.

4. Thompson AE, Shea B, Welch V, Fenlon D, Pope JE. Calcium-channel blockers for Raynaud's phenomenon in systemic sclerosis. Arthritis Rheum 2001:1841-1847.

5. Pope J, Fenlon D, Thompson A, Shea B, Furst D, Wells G, Silman A. Iloprost and cisaprost for Raynaud's phenomenon in progressive systemic sclerosis (Cochrane Review). In: The Cochrane Library, Issue 1, 2002. Oxford: Update Software.

6. Steen VD, Medsger TA. The value of the Health Assessment Questionnaire and special patient-generated scales to demonstrate change in systemic sclerosis patients over time. Arthritis Rheum 1997:1984-91.

7. Black C, Korn J, Mayes M, Matucci-Cerinic M, Rainisio M, Gaitonde M, et al. Prevention of ischemic digital ulcers in systemic sclerosis by endothelin receptor antagonism. (Late Breaking Oral Abstract presented at the ACR Annual Meeting, 2002). Arthritis Rheum 2002;46:3414.

[6] Approach to the systemically unwell patient
[a] Is it Vasculitis?
Dr. Avril Fitzgerald, University of Calgary

KEY CONCEPTS

You should suspect a Systemic Vasculitis in the following clinical scenarios:

- ▶ patient with multiple organ involvement which is difficult to explain by a single disease process
- ▶ systemic symptoms (eg fever, weight loss, cachexia) that cannot be explained after usual investigations
- ▶ organ ischemia or infarction (myocardial infarction, bowel infarction)
- ▶ finding a common condition (eg myocardial infarction, congestive heart failure) in an uncommon age group

1. Presentation of Systemic Vasculitides varies according to the size and distribution of the blood vessels in the disease process. A useful classification bases on size of vessels involved is shown in Fig. 1.

Figure 1. Range of vascular involvement by vasculitides

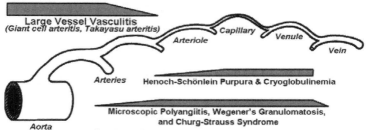

Small Vessel Vasculitis
(e.g. microscopic polyangiitis, Wegener's granulomatosis)

Medium-Sized Vessel Vasculitis
(Polyarteritis nodosa, Kawasaki disease)

Large Vessel Vasculitis
(Giant cell arteritis, Takayasu arteritis)

Capillary
Arteriole
Venule
Vein

Arteries **Henoch-Schönlein Purpura & Cryoglobulinemia**

Microscopic Polyangiitis, Wegener's Granulomatosis, and Churg-Strauss Syndrome

Aorta

Reproduced with permission J C Jennett, Arthritis & Rheumatism February 1994

2. Complete history and physical examination are instrumental to the diagnosis.

3. Laboratory results are sometimes helpful in differentiating one form of vasculitis from another, as well as EMG and angiography.

4. Biopsy, when possible, is very important to confirm the diagnosis and to help differentiate one form of systemic vasculitis from another.

5. A high index of suspicion is required to diagnose systemic vasculitis

6. Outcome of systemic vasculitis can be catastrophic and investigations and diagnosis must be completed in an expedient fashion.

History

Symptoms obtained in the history may be nonspecific, but the **pattern or constellation of symptoms** in a patient may help to raise suspicion of a systemic vasculitis and may also help in the differentiation of one systemic vasculitis from another. A previous history of drug exposure, history of hepatitis or risk behaviours or previous diagnosis of a CTD are important to ascertain. Complaints of fatigue, weakness, fever, arthralgias, abdominal pain, hypertension, renal insufficiency and neurologic dysfunction are particularly common.

Patient Demographics

This Table illustrates characteristic epidemiologic features of individual vasculitic syndromes as well as a general description of a typical case.

Sex	Age	Ethnic Assoc	Vasculitis	Clinical Characteristics
female=male	<5 years	Asian	Kawasaki's	Strawberry tongue, palmar desquamation, conjunctivitis, coronary artery aneurysm
female=male	<18 years	------	HSP	Palpable purpura, abdominal pain, arthritis, IgA nephropathy
female>male	<25 years	Asian/ Hispanic	Takayasu's	Pulselessness, fever, weight loss, hypertension, bruits
female=male	Young adult	-----	Cogan's syndrome	Keratitis, vestibulo-auditory loss
female<male	Middle age	-----	PAN	Chronic Hep B, weight loss, fever, myalgias, neuropathy, abdominal pain/ infarction
female=male	Middle age	----	WG	Sinusitis, rash, pulmonary infiltrates, arthritis, GN, cANCA
female=male	Middle age	----	MPA	Pulmonary hemorrhage, renal failure, pANCA
female=male	Middle age	----	CSS	Asthma, eosinophilia, IgE, arthritis, pANCA
female>male	>50 years	N. European	GCA	Polymyalgia rheumatica, ESR, scalp tenderness, headaches, visual loss, jaw claudication
female=male	<35 years	Middle Eastern	Behcet's	Oral/genital ulcers, thrombophlebitis, uveitis, folliculitis, CNS
female=male	Middle age	-------	Isolated Cerebral Angiitis	Headache, CNS abnormalities, cerebral vasculitis on angiogram
female<male	Adult	-----	Mixed cryoglobulinemia	Hep C, mixed cryoglobulins, GN, arthritis

Key Questions

Fever:

- ► Most important to rule out more common causes:
    - ►► bacterial, viral, fungal, mycobacterial infections
    - ►► Systemic causes: bacterial endocarditis, atrial myxoma, sarcoidosis
- ► Any systemic vasculitis/CTD especially SLE, PAN, WG, MPA, Takayasu's, GCA

Weight loss:

- ► Consider first primary metabolic and systemic or psychiatric conditions such as thyroid disease, diabetes, malabsorption, neoplasia, anorexia, depression.
- ► Any systemic vasculitis especially PAN, WG, CSS, MPA

Arthralgias/arthritis:

- ► Very common symptom in connective tissue diseases and systemic vasculitides (SLE, WG, CSS, PAN, HSP, MPA, Behcet's).
- ► Pattern of joint symptoms in systemic vasculitis is variable (small joint polyarthritis to larger joint mono/oligoarthritis) so pattern of joint pain is unlikely to help differentiate among CTDs or systemic vasculitides. Consider also common arthritides (RA, psoriatic, spondyloarthropathy).
- ► Consider infectious causes eg viral/bacterial infection, other systemic diseases, eg sarcoidosis, inflammatory bowel disease.

Headache:

- ► Common nonspecific symptom in patients generally, unless associated with scalp tenderness or localized temporal/occipital pain, jaw claudication.
- ► Consider GCA, SLE, Behcet's, Isolated Cerebral Angiitis

Raynauds Phenomenon:

- ► Most often is idiopathic but there is an increased association with CTDs (SLE, Systemic Sclerosis, Sjogren's, Dermatomyositis) and systemic vasculitides (PAN) and cryoglobulinemia.

Neuropathic Pain/Polyneuropathy/Mononeuritis Multiplex:

- ► Consider other systemic causes eg diabetes mellitus, B12 deficiency.
- ► Consider SLE, PAN, WG, CSS, MPA

Claudication:

► May relate to arterial insufficiency in conditions such as Takayasu's Arteritis, GCA, or arterial thrombosis of Behcet's or antiphospholipid antibody syndrome.

Confusion:

► Consider systemic illness, sepsis, metabolic causes.
► Consider SLE, Behcet's, Isolated Cerebral Angiitis

Reduced/Loss vision:

► Consider primary ocular diseases eg uveitis, retinitis, retinal detachment.
► Of the vasculitides consider particularly GCA, Behcet's, WG, Cogan's.

Sinusitis/Upper Respiratory Tract:

► Consider infectious, allergic causes first.
► Of the vasculitides consider particularly WG, Cogan's Syndrome.

Chest pain/cough/shortness of breath/hemoptysis:

► Consider other systemic diseases or infections eg pneumonia, pulmonary embolus.
► Recent onset asthma (especially with eosinophilia) strongly consider CSS
► SLE, PAN, CSS, WG, MPA, Goodpasture's
► Kawasaki's, Takayasu's, SLE

Abdominal Pain:

► Consider more common causes first (peptic ulcer disease, diverticulitis, peritonitis, surgical abdomen) and other systemic conditions (eg inflammatory bowel disease). Bowel ischemia/infarction may be cause in a patient with other multisytem symptoms that could suggest a systemic vasculitis.
► PAN, HSP
► SLE, Behcet's

PHYSICAL EXAMINATION

The diagnosis of a systemic vasculitis is often delayed because clinical features are seen in a number of disorders but some physical signs are particularly suggestive eg mononeuritis multiplex, palpable purpura. The pattern of organ involvement may suggest a certain vasculitis eg hemoptysis and renal disease - WG, MPA, SLE, Goodpasture's syndrome with a differential diagnosis of pulmonary infections and emboli.

Mucocutaneous Lesions:

Palpable purpura (leukocytoclastic vasculitis) differential diagnoses:
- ▶ Hypocomplementemic vasculitis
- ▶ Mixed cryoglobulinemia
- ▶ HSP
- ▶ SLE and other CTD

Livedo Reticularis (medium size muscular artery)
- ▶ PAN
- ▶ SLE/antiphospholipid antibody syndrome

Oral/Genital Ulcers, folliculitis, pathergy-- Behcet's

Desquamation palms/strawberry tongue-- Kawasaki's

Periungal erythema
- ▶ Non-specific but consider CTDs eg SLE, DM/PM, SSc
- ▶ Consider systemic vasculitides eg WG, CSS

Nonspecific vasculitic rashes: WG, CSS, SLE

Arthritis:

- ▶ SLE frequently associated with symmetrical, polyarticular small joints
- ▶ Arthritis of other systemic vasculitides may be more variable-- more larger joints in oligoarticular pattern,
- ▶ SLE, SP, WG, CSS, MPA, Behcet's

Pulmonary Disease:

- ▶ Hemoptysis: SLE, WG, CSS, MPA, Goodpasture's Syndrome
- ▶ Asthma: CSS
- ▶ Pulmonary Infiltrates: SLE, WG, CSS, MPA, PAN, Goodpasture's, Sarcoidosis

Glomerulonephritis:

► SLE, WG, MPA, HSP, CSS, mixed cryoglobulinemia, Goodpasture's

Hypertension (non-glomerulonephritis):

► Takayasu's, PAN

Peripheral Neuropathy/Mononeuritis Multiplex:

► SLE, PAN, WG, CSS, MPA

Central Nervous System:

► Consider underlying secondary metabolic/infectious/systemic complication

► Isolated cerebral angiitis, Behcet's, SLE, CSS

Ophthalmologic disease:

► Optic nerve ischemia-GCA

► Uveitis-Behcet's, WG, Sarcoidosis

► Scleritis-WG, Relapsing Polychondritis

KEY LABORATORY FINDINGS

WBC - frequently elevated with neutrophilia in systemic vasculitis (in contrast to leukopenia seen in active SLE), major differential diagnosis includes sepsis. Eosinophilia is seen in association with CSS.

ESR, CRP - nonspecific and frequently elevated

Urinalysis - look for proteinuria or active renal sediment suggesting a glomerulonephritis

Cryoglobulins - Blood proteins found in serum that precipitate at temperature <37°C. Immunoglobulins may be monoclonal (Type I) as seen in myeloma and Waldenstroms; or (Type II) a mixture of monoclonal and polyclonal Ig seen with viral infections such as Hep C and HIV; or polyclonal (Type III) seen in CTD.

Hepatitis serology - There is an increased association of Hepatitis B infection and PAN (?10%). Of patients with mixed cryoglobulinemia, approximately 90% have positive Hep C serology.

Antinuclear Antibodies - Useful as a screen for SLE but increased incidence of positive results in other systemic vasculitides. Extractable Nuclear Antibodies and Anti-DNA Antibodies may help to identify SLE, other specific CTDs or overlap syndromes.

C3, C4 - Reduced in cryoglobulinemia and some patients with active SLE.

ANCA - Anti-neutrophil Cytoplasmic Antibodies are assayed by indirect immunofluorescence (IIF) and are seen in the majority of patients with a systemic vasculitis (active WG 90%, MPA 70%, CSS 50%, Goodpasture's 10-40%). This test is not specific for vasculitis. False positives can be seen in other immune-mediated conditions such as other CTDs, inflammatory bowel disease (60%),autoimmune hepatitis or chronic infections. There are two patterns - cANCA (cytoplasmic antibodies that show diffuse staining throughout the cytoplasm) and pANCA (perinuclear antibodies that show staining around the nucleus). Interpretation of the significance of the ANCA result must be made in association with the ELISA and the clinical picture.   Serial changes in ANCA results may not correlate well with clinical remission or relapse in some patients and must be viewed with consideration of the clinical appearance of the patients.

Anti-PR3 - This antibody pattern, found by ELISA, correlates with cytoplasmic staining by IIF (cANCA). It is the most specific antibody pattern for WG (80-95%). It is very occasionally seen in patients who have clinical diagnoses of MPA, CSS and Goodpasture's syndrome.

Anti-MPO - This antibody pattern, found by ELISA, correlates with perinuclear staining by IIF (pANCA). It is seen commonly in association with MPA (50%) and CSS (60%), as well as some patients with WG, Goodpasture's syndrome or PAN.

	Microscopic Polyangiitis	Wegener's Granulomatosis	Churg-Strauss Syndrome
PR3-ANCA	40%	75%	10%
MPO-ANCA	50%	20%	60%
Negative	10%	5%	30%

adapted from Jennette JC Seminars in Diagnostic Pathology 2001

EMG - Useful in confirming myositis, neuropathy, mononeuritis multiplex.

EKG - May help detect myocardial ischemia, infarction, arrhythmia, pericardial effusion.

Arteriography/MR Angiogram - May help to identify medium and large artery involvement eg PAN, Takayasu's, GCA

Vasculitis Diagnostic Algorithm

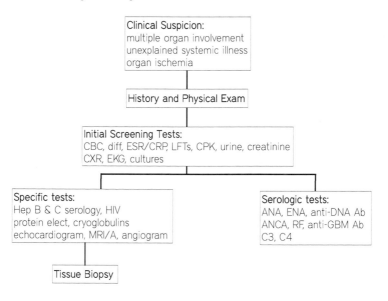

Clinical Suspicion:
multiple organ involvement
unexplained systemic illness
organ ischemia

History and Physical Exam

Initial Screening Tests:
CBC, diff, ESR/CRP, LFTs, CPK, urine, creatinine
CXR, EKG, cultures

Specific tests:
Hep B & C serology, HIV
protein elect, cryoglobulins
echocardiogram, MRI/A, angiogram

Serologic tests:
ANA, ENA, anti-DNA Ab
ANCA, RF, anti-GBM Ab
C3, C4

Tissue Biopsy

Pathology

Below is shown a representation of the pathologic findings in the systemic vasculitides as determined by the size and type of vessel involvement, type of cell infiltration and presence of immune deposits or other characteristic pathologic features as illustrated by Dr Jennette.

From Jennett JC Seminars in Diagnostic Pathology 2001

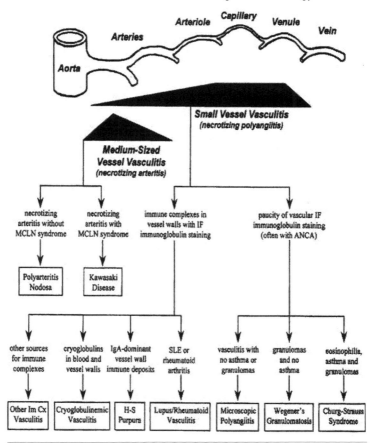

	Henoch-Schonlein Purpura	Cryoglobulinemic Vasculitis	Microscopic Polyangiitis	Wegener's Granulomatosis	Churg Strauss Syndrome
Small-vessel vasculitis signs and symptoms	+	+	+	+	+
IgA-dominant immune deposits	+	O	O	O	O
Cryoglobulins in blood and Ovessels	O	+	O	O	O
ANCA in blood	O	O	+	+	+
Necrotizing granuloma	O	O	O	+	+
Asthma and eosinophilia	O	O	O	O	+

From Jennett JC Seminars in Diagnostic Path 2001

KEY CONCEPTS IN THERAPY OF VASCULITIS

The treatment of systemic vasculitis is dependent on the specific diagnosis. Some conditions respond readily to relatively low doses of corticosteroid therapy, some require high dose steroids and other require more aggressive immune modulating therapy to achieve a clinical remission. Biologic agents (infliximab, etanercept, campath 1H, interferon α, rituximab) have been tried in small uncontrolled trials in several vasculitic syndromes. It is probable that some of these will have future roles in the treatment of systemic vasculitis.

Other factors that may determine which therapy is used include the severity of the illness, which particular organs are affected, concomitant illnesses and the ability of the patient to tolerate specific therapies. Consultation with a Rheumatologist should always be sought when managing patients with vasculitis.

Cutaneous vasculitis

Corticosteroids, orally in low dose or as a steroid ointment may be effective in treating some cutaneous vasculitic syndromes such as a leukocytoclastic rash associated with a drug reaction, infection or malignancy. Dapsone and colchicine have also been used for leukocytoclastic vasculitis. Leukocytoclastic vasculitis associated with Hepatitis C is best treated with anti-viral therapy such as interferon and ribaviron.

HSP

HSP usually responds to corticosteroids in children and adults although patients can develop complications of glomerulonephritis or intra-abdominal complications

Giant Cell Arteritis/Takayasu's

Corticosteroids alone are very effective in treatment of GCA when given in reducing doses over a one-to-two year period.
Steroids may be of possible benefit in Takayasu's Arteritis and the outcome of Takayasu's has not been shown to improve with the use of cytotoxic agents. Arterial by-pass procedure is often successful to bypass critical narrowing of arteries in Takayasu's.

Wegener's Granulomatosis

Survival of patients with WG was not substantially improved with the introduction of corticosteroids (50% survival at 1 year) but a significant improvement in prognosis was observed with the use of cyclophosphamide (80% at 8 years). In WG, cyclophosphamide is given daily orally or intermittent intravenous infusions for remission induction therapy, usually for the first six months. Cyclophosphamide is then withdrawn in favor of methotrexate for maintenance of remission. Corticosteroids are weaned over the first three to six months of treatment. Risk of hemorrhagic cystitis with cyclophosphamide is reduced with the concomitant use of Mesna when cyclophosphamide is given intravenously. Use of concomitant prophylactic antibiotic therapy (Septra three times weekly) is recommended to reduce the risk of opportunistic infections while on cyclophosphamide.

Prognosis for PAN and MPA is generally worse that WG and treatment must include concomitant corticosteroid and cyclophosphamide therapy. Methotrexate has not been found to be a suitable remission- maintenance therapy in these vasculitis syndromes, and these conditions frequently relapse. It is important to aggressively treat non-glomerulonephritis associated hypertension in these conditions.

Kawasaki's Disease

Patients with Kawasaki's arteritis are treated with high dose salicylate therapy to reduce incidence of coronary artery aneurysms. Patients often respond dramatically to intravenous gammaglobulin especially when given within the first week of disease onset.

Behcet's Disease

Orogenital lesions are treated with local application of corticosteroids. Mucocutaneous manifestations and arthritis in Behcet's often respond to the use of colchicine. Corticosteroids are indicated for the treatment of Behcet's but this has not been reported in controlled studies. The combination of corticosteroids and immunosuppressant therapy is used when vital organs are involved. Azathioprine and cyclosporine have been used. Cyclosporine alone or combined with azathioprine is effective in severe uveitis. Pulse cyclophosphamide with steroids is used in the treatment of severe vasculitis and CNS Behcet's.

Goodpasture's Syndrome

Treatment of choice is plasmapheresis in combination with corticosteroids and cyclophosphamide.

CSS

Corticosteroids in high dose are often sufficient for CSS except if there is evidence of cardiac or neurologic involvement when the addition of a cytotoxic agent such as cyclophosphamide may be indicated.

REFERENCES

1. Centers for Disease Control. Kawasaki disease - New York. MMWR Morb Mortal Wkly Rep 1980; 29:61

2. Hunder GG et al. The American College of Rheumatology 1990 criteria for the classification of vasculitis. Arthritis Rheum 1990; 33:1065 (see also pp 1129 (Takayasu), 1122 (Giant Cell arteritis), 1101 (Wegener's granulomatosis), 1088 (Polyarteritis nodosa), 1094 (Churg-Strauss syndrome))

3. Jennette JC et al.   Small-vessel vasculitis. N Engl J Med 1997; 337:1512.

4. Jennette JC et al.   Microscopic Polyantiitis. Seminars in Diagnostic Pathology 2001;18(1):3-13.

5. Kallenberg CG et al. Anti-neutophil cyctoplasmic antibodies: Current diagnostic and pathophysiologic potential. Kidney Int 1994; 46:1.

6. Michel BA et al. Hypersensitivity vasculitis and Henoch-Schonlein pur-pura: A comparison between the 2 disorders.   J Rheumatol 1992; 19:721.

[6] Approach to the systemically unwell patient
[b] Is it a Collagen Vascular Disease?
Dr. Paul Davis, University of Alberta

KEY CONCEPTS

▶ Multisystem connective tissue diseases (collagen vascular diseases) compromise a heterogeneous group of conditions including systemic lupus erythematosus, progressive systemic sclerosis (scleroderma), mixed connective tissue disease, polymyositis/dermatomyositis and Sjogren's syndrome.

▶ These diseases are generally characterized by sustained, systemic inflammation (scleroderma may be inflammatory early in the disease process, but most disease manifestations are due to tissue fibrosis and/or vasculopathy)

▶ Early undifferentiated disease may be manifested by common features of arthritis, serositis, small vessel vasculitis, skin rash, myositis and systemic manifestations of fever, weight loss and fatigue. Nonspecific inflammatory markers such as anemia, elevated ESR and CRP and markers of autoreactivity such ANA may be present.

▶ Over time, most evolve to a specific syndrome with a characteristic clinical picture and autoantibody profile.

▶ Those who show distinct features of two or more diseases may be characterized as having an overlap syndrome.

Brief Descriptions

▶ Systemic lupus erythematosus is an autoimmune disease characterized by loss of tolerance to cellular antigens, most notably nuclear ones. Clinical features occur as a result of immune mediated inflammation due to in situ or circulating immune complex deposition.

▶ Systemic sclerosis (scleroderma) is characterized by the production and tissue deposition of abnormal and/or excessive quantities of collagen. Clinical features can usually be attributed to tissue fibrosis and/or an associated vasculopathy (non-inflammatory, structural and functional vascular abnormalities).

▶ Polymyositis, dermatomyositis and inclusion body myositis are inflammatory disorders of skeletal muscle with or without skin involvement. Each has characteristic clinical features, histopathology and immune markers (see section 2:4).

▶ Sjogren's syndrome is a cell mediated autoimmune disorder of exocrine glands. Clinical features can usually be predicted on the basis of reduced volume and/or increased viscosity of exocrine secretions. The commonest manifestations are keratoconjunctivitis sicca ("dry eyes") and xerostomia ("dry mouth")

▶ Mixed connective tissue disease is characterized by the presence of elements of SLE, inflammatory myositis and scleroderma, and a particular autoantibody profile (anti-RNP). While similar to an overlap syndrome, many consider this to be a distinct clinical entity.

Diagnosis

▶ In all conditions, the disease may be insidious in onset consequently leading to delay in diagnosis.

▶ In contrast, some patients present with acute manifestations of the condition which often constitutes a rheumatologic medical emergency.

▶ Specific documentation of disease manifestations need to be clearly determined over time as witnessed by a physician.

▶ Many manifestations are nonspecific and can consequently lead to confusion in differential diagnosis,

▶ The pattern of organ system involvement may help define a specific diagnosis.

▶ A complete medical history is essential

HISTORY

Patient Demographics

These conditions frequently present in young or middle aged females, although none of them are age and sex specific.

Key Questions

Do you have...

- ▶ Constitutional symptoms:
    - ▸ Constitutional symptoms (weight loss, fatigue, low-grade fever, arthralgia, myalgia) are common but nonspecific.
- ▶ Arthralgias/Arthritis
- ▶ Raynaud's Phenomenon
- ▶ Skin rash or other skin/nail fold/fingertip lesions, "puffy" hands
- ▶ Oral ulcers, alopecia
- ▶ Muscle weakness
- ▶ Dry eyes/dry mouth:
    - ▸ Eyes gritty, thick discharge
    - ▸ Difficulty eating without liquids, water needed at bedside, increased dental caries
- ▶ Serositis- pleuritic chest pain, nonspecific abdominal pain

Past Medical History

A careful past medical history is important as previous medical conditions or events may not have been recognized for their significance. A careful review of past medical records and investigations is often helpful.

Family History

Family history is rarely of significance in making the clinical diagnosis.

PHYSICAL EXAMINATION

The pattern of organ system involvement over time may help make a specific diagnosis.

It is important to recognize that specific features of the organ system involved must be determined for accurate disease diagnosis and these findings documented by a physician. The distribution of organ involvement by disease is summarized in Table 1.

Organ System	Lupus	Scleroderma	Polymyositis/ Dermatomyositis	Sjogren's
Locomotor	Non-erosive synovitis Avascular necrosis Jaccouds arthritis	Puffy, shiny hands (early) Joint (tendon) contractures	Muscle wasting, weakness & tenderness	Arthralgia
Muco-cutaneous	Discoid LE Malar (butterfly) rash Alopecia Photosensitivity Oral ulcers Conjunctivitis	Digital pits Sclerodactyly Scleroderma Calcinosis Telangiectasia	Gottrens papules Heliotropic rash Periungual vasculitis	Dry mucous membranes xerophthalmia xerostomia reduced GI, pulmonary and genital secretions
Renal	Nephrotic syndrome Glomerulonephritis Renal failure	Acute renal failure(Scleroderma renal crisis with raised BP)		
CNS	Seizure disorder Psychiatric disorders			
Cardio-vascular	Raynaud's Pericarditis Endocarditis (Libman Sacks), Premature coronary artery disease, Secondary hypertension, Vasculitis Vascular thrombosis (antiphospholipid antibody syndrome)	Raynaud's Vasculopathy *Restrictive cardio-myopathy (2° to ischemia) *Pulmonary hypertension	Cardiomyopathy	
Pulmonary	Pleurisy & effusion Pneumonitis Pulmonary hemorrhage	Pulmonary fibrosis Pulmonary hypertension		Interstitial lung disease
Gastro-intestinal		Dysphagia,reflux Small bowel dysmotility and pseudo-obstruction		
Hemato-logic	Cytopenias Antiphospholipid antibody syndrome			Lymphoma

Vitals: Look for tachycardia (pericarditis, myocarditis, anemia etc.), tachypnea, fever, hypertension.

Head and neck: alopecia, ocular inflammation, oral and nasal ulcerations, malar rash, telangiectasia, lymphadenopathy

Chest: crackles (interstitial lung disease), rubs pleural effusions

CVS: rubs, CHF, signs of pulmonary hypertension

MSK: synovitis, check for muscle weakness

Derm: rashes, purpura, nodules, examine fingertips for pits, periungual erythema, telangiectasia, hemorrhages or infarcts

Additional notes:

▶ Manifestations of disease may only appear over time.

▶ Sjogren's syndrome can be associated with other rheumatologic disorders.

▶ Antiphospholipid antibody syndrome can occur as a primary disorder or in association with other connective tissue disease, most notably SLE.

▶ Myositis may be associated with malignancies.

KEY LABORATORY INVESTIGATIONS

▶ Investigations should be targeted to the specific organ systems clinically involved.

▶ Very few investigations are specific to the underlying condition with the exception of some nuclear autoantibodies.

▶ Some tests are as important for the monitoring of drug therapy toxicity as they are for the disease they treat.

The following is a list of investigations of particular importance and their value in the specific conditions (in brackets):

▶ **CBC, platelet count and differential** - cytopenias (SLE), eosinophilia (various connective tissue diseases, vasculitis)

▶ **Urea, electrolytes and urinalysis** - features of azotemia in acute or chronic renal failure (SLE and scleroderma), features of membranous or proliferative glomerulonephritis (SLE),

▶ **Muscle enzymes** - manifestation of myositis (polymyositis),

► **Antibodies to specific nuclear antigens** - characteristic of certain of the conditions with varying specificity and sensitivity (see section 3:9)

➤ ANA - nonspecific, may be present in any collagen vascular disease

➤ **Anti-Sm, anti-double stranded DNA** - specific to SLE

➤ **Anti-Ro/La** - associated with Sjogren's, also seen in SLE

➤ **Anti-RNP** - associated with Mixed Connective Tissue Disease

➤ **Anti-Jo-1** - associated with lung involvement in myositis

➤ **Anti-Scl70, anti-centromere antibody** - associated with diffuse and limited scleroderma respectively

► **Complement levels** - reduced in complement activation and immune complex formation (SLE),

► **EKG** - evidence of pericarditis (SLE)

► **Chest Xray** - features of pleurisy with pleural effusion (SLE), pulmonary fibrosis, (scleroderma)

► **Echocardiogram** - pulmonary hypertension (scleroderma), pericardial effusion (SLE).

► **Tissue Biopsy** - renal (SLE, scleroderma), muscle (polymyositis), salivary gland (Sjogren's), skin (SLE, dermatomyositis).

The following tests have low discriminatory value in distinguishing the multisystem connective tissue disease one from the other and include: liver function tests, serum urate, ESR, CRP, Rheumatoid factor, antinuclear antibody.

TREATMENT - KEY CONCEPTS

► The diversity and complexity of organ system involvement requires that each case needs to be treated individually.

► No one therapy is optimum for all.

► Monotherapy where possible to minimize drug side effects.

► Combination therapy may be required for multi system disease once having evaluated benefit to risk ratio.

► Drug/drug interaction and drug side effects can significantly add to the complexity of disease management.

► The evolution of the disease and its manifestations over time necessitates regular review of pharmacotherapy.

► Essential to appropriately monitor all drugs for side effects over time, and institute prophylaxis where appropriate (eg. for steroid-induced osteoporosis)

GENERAL APPROACH TO THERAPY

The following therapies have proven value in certain clinical situations:

▶ Topical preparations - sunscreens and steroid creams are of value in the management of cutaneous manifestations of lupus. Artificial tears are helpful for keratoconjunctivitis sicca.

▶ NSAIDs and analgesics - useful for nonspecific symptomatic relief of musculoskeletal symptoms, mild pericarditis.

▶ Steroids (oral and systemic) - often provide first line therapy for many of the inflammatory manifestations of the various diseases including arthritis, pleuritis, pericarditis, nephrotic syndrome or myositis. Are of value as a single agent or in combination with immunosuppressives for nephritis. Avoid "shotgun" approach of introducing steroids before every effort has been made to establish the diagnosis. In a patient with organ- or life-threatening disease, steroids may need to be introduced while investigations are ongoing. (See also section 4:11).

▶ Anti-malarials - of particular value in mild lupus limited to skin and joint disease and in DM for the skin involvement.

▶ Immunosuppressives - **Cyclophosphamide** as a single agent or in combination with steroids is of value for proliferative glomerulonephritis, pulmonary hemorrhage. Potential benefit in the suppression of the parenchymal pulmonary manifestations of systemic sclerosis. **Imuran** and **methotrexate** in combination with steroids are of value in many of these diseases as part of initial therapy or for "steroid sparing" effect. **Mycophenalate Mofetil (Cellcept)** - has an evolving role in the management of SLE, especially lupus nephritis.

SPECIAL SITUATIONS

▶ Antiphospholipid syndrome (primary or secondary): anticoagulation

▶ Raynaud's phenomenon (primary or secondary): see section 2:5

▶ Pulmonary hypertension (systemic sclerosis): IV epoprostenol or Bosentan (Tracleer)

▶ Malignant hypertension (systemic sclerosis): ACE inhibitors See section 5:15

▶ Keratoconjunctivitis sicca (Sjogren's syndrome): artificial moisture replacement (eg. Tears Naturale), pilocarpine (Salogen)

PROGNOSIS

▶ Careful treatment plans and the availability of new therapies have been associated with improved prognosis in both the short and long term.

▶ Long term prognosis may be influenced by evolving features of the disease eg. premature coronary artery disease in SLE, or by side effects of long term drug therapy (especially infection). Important to monitor closely and institute pre-emptive therapy/ prophylaxis where appropriate.

REFERENCES

▶ Primer on the Rheumatic Diseases (see full reference in Introduction)

▶ Chapters on Systemic Lupus Erythematosus, Systemic Sclerosis and Related Syndromes, Inflammatory and Metabolic Diseases of Muscle and Sjogren's Syndrome.

[7] Approach to Back Pain
Dr. Lori Albert, University of Toronto

Key Concepts

1. Low back pain is common and can be disabling

2. Typically seen in active, otherwise healthy people. It is not a feature of rheumatoid (or other seropositive) arthritis

3. Look for red flags to guide further investigations

4. In the absence of red flags, patients can be treated conservatively with physiotherapy, self-directed exercise, analgesics as needed, and the majority will improve

HISTORY

Demographics

60-80% of adults will suffer from at least one episode of back pain during their lifetime.

Risk factors include older age, heavy labour, especially jobs requiring lifting in an awkward position, lower education and income, smoking and obesity.

Prior episodes of back pain are strong predictors of recurrence.

Age over 50 or under 20 should raise increase index of suspicion for possible tumor or infection.

KEY QUESTIONS

The pathophysiology of most non-specific back pain is not well understood (but does not alter the management approach). Therefore, in evaluating patients presenting with low back pain, you should focus on determining:

1. Does the patient need emergency surgery (cauda equina syndrome, expanding vascular aneurysm with rupture or dissection)?

2. Does the patient have signs of nerve root compression ?

3. Is there an underlying medical cause of back pain (infectious, inflammatory, metabolic, tumor, visceral problem)-identified by presence of "red flags"?

HPI

What are your symptoms?

- ▶ Pain - back, leg or both? (consider nerve root compression with leg pain)

- ▶ Numbness (consider neurologic compromise)

- ▶ Stiffness (consider inflammatory back disease)

- ▶ Constant vs intermittent/situational (think more serious cause)

- ▶ Night or recumbency pain (consider tumor,infection)

- ▶ Is pain relieved by rest ? (failure of bed rest to relieve the pain is sensitive for systemic disease)

- ▶ Recent onset bladder dysfunction such as urinary retention, increased frequency or overflow incontinence ? (indicative of cauda equina syndrome)

► Is there saddle anaesthesia or severe or progressive neurological deficit in the lower extremity? (cauda equina)

When did the current limitations begin?

► Activities limited more than 4 weeks? (if greater than three months, think inflammatory process)

► How do your symptoms limit you?

► How long can you sit, stand, walk?

Have you had similar episodes previously?

► Previous testing or treatment?

Are there:

► Constitutional symptoms such as fever, chills or unexplained weight loss? (consider tumor or infection)

► Risk factors for spinal infection? - recent UTI (especially in elderly), iv drug abuse, immune suppression (steroids, transplant, HIV)

► History of major trauma (MVA or fall from height)

► Minor trauma or even strenuous lifting (in older or potentially osteoporotic individuals)

Pearl:

Summary of screening for ankylosing spondylitis

1. Is there morning stiffness?
2. Is there improvement in discomfort with exercise?
3. Was the onset of back pain before age 40?
4. Insidious onset?
5. Duration >3 months?

At least 4 positive answers has sensitivity of 0.95 and specificity of 0.85 (but predictive value may be low because of relative rarity of disease).

PMH

► Personal history of cancer (even if remote)?

▶ Risk factors for infection (vide supra)

▶ Risk factors for osteoporosis (esp. in elderly)

▶ Inflammatory bowel disease, iritis, psoriasis

MEDS

▶ Coumadin- consider bleed into cord, retroperitoneal bleed

▶ Immunosuppressives- consider epidural abscess

FH

Family history of spondylarthropathy, psoriasis or inflammatory bowel disease can all be relevant to a presenting complaint suggesting inflammatory back disease.

PHYSICAL EXAMINATION

General appearance: sick or well, degree of pain, exaggerated pain behaviour

Vital signs: Febrile, tachycardic consider infection

Head and neck: ocular inflammation, oral ulcers, psoriasis in scalp (all with seronegative disease)

Chest: Chest wall tenderness, sternomanubrial tenderness, reduced chest wall expansion (seronegative disease)

CVS: Asymmetrical pulses may indicate aortic dissection or indicate vascular claudication as a cause of leg pain

Abdomen: tenderness or enlargement of viscera may be cause of pain. Enlarged aneurysm may be cause

Back exam:

1. Regional back exam
2. Neurologic screening
3. Test for sciatic nerve tension

Inflammatory back exam will be reviewed at the end

1. Regional back exam:

▶ look for limping, coordination suggesting neurologic impairment

▶ Vertebral point tenderness to palpation may suggest spinal fracture/infection/tumor with the associated clinical picture

▶ Range of motion (flexion,extension, lateral flexion) - if guarding in all planes of movement, may suggest an infection, tumor or fracture (but this is not reliable unless very strong supporting clinical picture)

2. Neurologic examination

▶ focus on a few tests to look for nerve root impairment, peripheral neuropathy or spinal cord dysfunction

Pearl: >90 % of clinically significant lower extremity radiculopathies involve the L5 or S1 nerve root at the L4-5 or L5-S1 disc level

Nerve root	L4	L5	S1
Pain	Anterolateral thigh and shin	Buttock,lateral thigh and leg,dorsum foot	Buttock, back of thigh and leg, lateral foot
Numbness Screening:	PP on medial aspect of foot	PP on dorsal foot	PP on lateral aspect of foot
Motor weakness	Extension of quadriceps	Dorsiflexion of great toe and foot	Plantar flexion of great toe and foot
Screening exam	Squat and rise	Supine pt dorsiflexes ankle against examiner's resistance. Also, "point your toe at your nose" and resist with two fingers	Toe walking/ hamstring and hip extensor strength
Reflexes	Knee jerk diminished	None reliable (sometimes adductor reflex if absent on affected side)	Ankle jerk diminished

Presence of up-going toes (positive Babinski) may indicate upper motor-neuron abnormalities (such as myelopathy or demyelinating disease).

Look for evidence of muscle atrophy by comparing circumferential measurements of calf and thigh bilaterally- asymmetry will be seen in neurologic impairment or if there is a pre-existing joint problem (eg. hamstring and anterior compartment wasting for longstanding S1 root injuries).

Look for saddle anesthesia- buttocks, posterior-superior thighs and perineal region. Also assess for reduced anal sphincter tone if indicated.

3. Tests for sciatic nerve tension

Straight leg raising a) supine
                           b) sitting

a) *Supine:* cup heel in one hand and keeping the knee fully extended with other, slowly raise the straight leg from the examining table until pain occurs.

Tension is transmitted to the nerve roots once the leg is raised beyond 30 but after 70 further movement of the nerve is negligible, and movement of the pelvis occurs because of stretch of the hamstrings.

A positive test reproduces sciatica symptoms between 30 and 60 degrees of leg elevation.

Can confirm a positive test by dorsiflexing the foot, which should aggravate symptoms, even if the elevation of the foot is reduced by 10-15 degrees. Reproduction of pain in the back with SLR is not a positive test. Final phase of testing involves dorsiflexing foot after reducing elevation of the foot by further 10-15°. This should not aggravate symptoms as tension has been reduced on nerve.

A crossed SLR occurs when SLR is performed on the unaffected leg, and is found to elicit pain in the symptomatic leg.

b) *Sitting:* With patient sitting on a table, both hip and knees flexed at 90 degrees, slowly extend the knee. This maneuver stretches nerve roots and the patient with significant nerve root irritation will complain or lean backward to reduce tension on the nerve.

Back examination for inflammatory spondyloarthropathy

▶ Range of motion lumbar spine may be reduced with spondylitis

    » Schober test- place a mark with a pen at lumbosacral junction (dimples of Venus) and a mark 10cm above

    » With forward flexion distance between marks should increase to 15cm

    » Reduction in other planes of movement of lumbar spine can be monitored, Eg. Measure finger-fibula distance for lateral flexion

- Thoraco-lumbar rotation may be reduced with spondylitis
  - ▸ Patient sitting on bed, arms crossed to opposite shoulders, assess rotation by bringing each shoulder forward to midline in turn. Normal range 60-90°
- Reduced range of motion of cervical spine
- Reduced chest expansion
  - ▸ Patient places hands on head, place tape measure at nipple line (T4)
  - ▸ Inhale-exhale- measure movement from end-expiration to end-inspiration. Normal 5-6 cm
- Stress maneuvers for sacroiliac joints:
  - ▸ FABER (flexion,abduction and external rotation with distracting force)
  - ▸ Gaenslen's (hyperextension of hip/leg of supine patient over edge of bed produces pain in ipsilateral SI joint, while pelvis is stabilized by patient holding flexed knee against chest on contralateral side)
  - ▸ Direct compression over SI joints
  - ▸ Lateral compression- examiner places weight through extended arms on lateral pelvis of patient in side-lying position. Pain in inferior SI joint (side on the table)

All of these tests are poorly reproducible and inaccurate in distinguishing inflammatory from mechanical spine problems.

Always check for **enthesitis** eg. heel pain at Achilles insertion or plantar fascia insertion or tenderness at pelvic brim when assessing for seronegative disease.

KEY LABORATORY TESTING

In a patient in whom mechanical back pain is less likely (>age 50 or concerning features on history or physical):

CBC
ESR (look for very high ESR suggesting malignancy or infection)
ALP, Calcium
Serum protein electrophoresis
Urine/blood cultures if indicated
HLAB27 testing is rarely helpful in the setting of back pain

KEY IMAGING

► Plain Xray can be very helpful in setting of subacute back pain - rarely of help in acute back pain unless history of trauma or high index of suspicion for pathologic fracture (although this may not even show up on plain Xray)

► Bone scan - may show recent fracture, focal inflammatory process (infection, tumor), does not reliably show lytic lesions unless there is an osteoblastic reaction; may show changes of inflammatory back disease

► CT scan - better for seeing bone than MRI

► MRI - better defines soft tissue in setting of suspect disc herniation, paraspinal disease

⇥ THE test if cauda equina or myelopathy suspected

DIFFERENTIAL DIAGNOSIS

Differential diagnosis of back pain discussed above.
Conditions which may mimic back pain:

► Disease of visceral organs

► Dissecting aneurysm

► Myocardial infarction

TREATMENT OPTIONS

► To review an algorithm for management

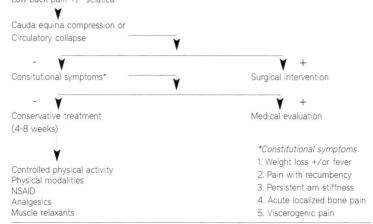

Low back pain +/- sciatica
↓
Cauda equina compression or
Circulatory collapse ———→ → + Surgical intervention

- ↓
Consitutional symptoms* ———→ → + Medical evaluation

- ↓
Conservative treatment
(4-8 weeks)

↓

Controlled physical activity
Physical modalities
NSAID
Analgesics
Muscle relaxants

*Constitutional symptoms
1. Weight loss +/or fever
2. Pain with recumbency
3. Persistent am stiffness
4. Acute localized bone pain
5. Viscerogenic pain

- ▶ Treatment of infection, malignant lesion depends on the nature of the process, and should be undertaken with the input of the appropriate consultants.

- ▶ Treatment of osteoporotic fracture usually conservative. Miacalcin nasal spray (calcitonin) 200 IU once daily X 4-6 weeks can diminish pain of an acute fracture

- ▶ Treatment of spondyloarthropathy initially consists of physiotherapy and NSAIDs (traditionally Indocid, naproxen). Steroids rarely indicated. Referral to rheumatologist appropriate for further management.

REFERENCES

The Back guide, www.backguide.com
Institute for Work and Health, 1999.

Deyo R., et al. JAMA 1992; 268:760-765.

[8] Approach to Rheumatic manifestations of medical diseases

[a] Rheumatic Manifestations of HIV/AIDS

Dr. Michael Blackmore, University of Toronto

KEY CONCEPTS

1. Various reports estimate that between 40-60 million people world-wide have been affected by HIV with an increasing incidence in third world countries.

2. Rheumatic manifestations of HIV/AIDS occur in up to 65% of patients.

3. Musculoskeletal disease may occur at any time during the clinical spectrum of HIV/AIDS but tends to increase in frequency and severity with the severity of the HIV infection.

4. These rheumatologic complaints range from severe arthropathies to myalgias to opportunistic infections. Rheumatoid arthritis and typical connective tissue diseases tend NOT to occur.

5. Antiretroviral therapy (HAART) has prolonged life spans but is now implicated in new and unusual rheumatologic manifestations.

6. Treatment of muscle and joint pains may be complicated by immuno-supression or HAART interactions.

7. In any person presenting with a new non-RA/SLE arthritis or MSK problem, think of HIV; is there a history of IV drug use? Has there been a history of multiple sexual partners or unprotected sex? Discuss openly and gently with patient about HIV testing.

HISTORY

Patient Demographics

► High risk groups include patients with multiple sexual partners or with history of unprotected sex.

► Remember men and women, STRAIGHT and GAY can be infected.

► HIV has become almost ENDEMIC in South East Asia and Africa.

► IV drug abusers and hemophiliacs or anyone receiving blood products prior to testing should be thought of.

Key Questions

► Clarify if true arthritis(synovitis) with painful stiffness and swelling vs. diffuse muscle aches.

► Acute symptoms vs. prolonged

► Duration of HIV/AIDS and the current CD4/viral load

► Antiretroviral therapy vs. untreated

► Extraarticular features (psoriasis, iritis, fever or other infectious symptoms etc.)

Disease Patterns

I. Related primarily to HIV/AIDS

► First reported cases in 1980's include Psoriatic Arthritis and Reactive Arthritis with severe joint destruction and extraarticular features. Very difficult to treat in view of immunosupression. Now VERY uncommon with HAART

► Painful Articular Syndrome: acutely painful joints; maybe polyarticular and resemble crystalline arthropathy

► Arthralgias and myalgias of a non-specific nature are very common. There are no diagnostic tests for this.

► Infectious Arthritis actually NOT that common and when does occur is often unusual i.e. Fungal, TB etc. Much more common bacterial septic joints more likely seen in drug abusers e.g. Staph and Strep infectious arthritis

► Typical inflammatory Polymyositis and Dermatomyositis have been reported but are rare

▶ Infectious muscle disease, pyomyositis may occur but is not common. Present with severe pain localized to one muscle area. There may be minimal diagnostic features with early presentation.

▶ A syndrome resembling Sjogren's Syndrome has been seen in severe cases of AIDS. The lymphoproliferation is severe resulting in huge salivary gland enlargement. This syndrome has been named Diffuse Infiltrative Lymphocytosis Syndrome

▶ Miscellaneous conditions include any and all forms of vasculitis and hypertrophic osteoarthropathy

▶ SLE and RA are rarely reported with HIV- probably because these diseases are CD4 dependent. In fact some literature suggests these conditions may IMPROVE after HIV infection

II. **Related to Prolonged HIV Illness and Stable HIV/AIDS patients on antiretroviral therapy**

▶ Fibromyalgia - Initial studies showed increased incidence of this condition in HIV-infected people. With increased survival on HAART the incidence is increased. This author finds FM in MOST people with HIV despite disease duration (no published data).

▶ Avascular Necrosis -   increasingly reported and may or may not be related to HAART. To date no evidence to suggest this is related to anti-cardiolipin antibodies found in HIV positive people.

▶ AZT and other HAART therapy known to cause MYOPATHY and NEUROPATHY

▶ Osteoporosis- now found increasingly in HIV-infected patients with some data to suggest it may be related to therapy

▶ Crystalline arthropathies- increasingly being seen in association with HAART. Whether caused by these therapies or not remains controversial

▶ Rotator cuff tendonitis, lateral epicondylitis and other tendonopathies - seen frequently with HAART. These are NOT the same as the characteristic ENTHESOPATHIES of the seronegative arthropathies seen with untreated HIV e.g. Achilles tendonitis.

There is usually less inflammation and the locations are more typical of common tendonopathies eg. tennis elbow.

INVESTIGATIONS

As with any form of arthritis - appropriate blood work (CBC, liver enzymes, creatinine, septic work-up, ESR) and Xrays (see sections 2:1, 2 and section 3).

Ultrasound, bone scan may help to sort out true inflammatory conditions from FM and non-specific myalgias.

Bone scan and/or MRI will confirm AVN

As with any mono- or oligo-arthritis, aspirate any swollen joints. Test for the usual eg. cell count, and crystals AND ALWAYS test for infection including mycobacterium and fungi.

Screen for other sexually transmitted diseases such as gonorrhea, chlamydia and syphilis which are reported to be increasing in frequency.

TREATMENT

▶ TREAT the HIV infection. Outcomes are better particularly with regard to the seronegative diseases like Psoriatic Arthritis and Reactive Arthritis. (Though there are no long-term prospective trials).

▶ Supportive measures such as education regarding joint protection and exercise. Physiotherapy may prove invaluable particularly in otherwise untreatable conditions like avascular necrosis or fibromyalgia

▶ NSAIDS and COX-2 inhibitors are very useful and do not interact with HAART'S

▶ Use of immunosuppressives is still controversial. Always be aware of the patient's degree of immunosupression from HIV. Sulfasalazine, Methotrexate and Azathioprine have been used but should only be reserved for the most CRITICAL of Rheumatologic diseases.

▶ TREAT Fibromyalgia like Fibromyalgia- exercise, counseling and typical low dose tricyclic antidepressants

HIV

SUMMARY

► Rheumatic manifestations are very common in HIV/AIDS

► These manifestations may occur both early in the course of AIDS or after years of living with the virus

► HAART has resulted in less likelihood of the severe erosive arthropathies such as Psoriatic Arthritis

► Recent changes in the face of the disease have resulted in findings of eminently treatable conditions such as tendonopathies and osteoporosis

► Always think of Fibromyalgia

► Treatment may be extremely helpful but caution needs to be kept in mind with respect to immunosuppressive drugs for Psoriatic Arthritis or Reactive Arthritis

KEY REFERENCES

Rodriguez, F. M.,Rheum Dis Clin N Am 29 (2003) 145-161

Vassilopoulos D. and Calabrese L. H., Clev Clin J of Med 65 #8 (1998) 436-431

[8] Approach to Rheumatic manifestations of medical diseases
[b] Is This Patient at Risk for Osteoporosis?

Dr. Heather McDonald-Blumer, University of Toronto

KEY CONCEPTS

Preamble

It is rare that patients will attend an acute care hospital or emergency department with a presenting complaint of osteoporosis aside from seeing the emergency physician or orthopaedic surgeon for acute fracture care. However, for those of us practicing internal medicine, recognition and care of patients with osteoporosis can be part of daily practice. It has to be "on your radar screen" and where relevant, should be part of optimal patient care. Remember, the clinical outcome of concern with osteoporosis is the occurrence of low trauma fractures which carry with them a significant morbidity and mortality.

Key Concepts

The diagnosis of osteoporosis is made by assessing the information obtained from the patient's history, physical examination and review of radiographic studies such as thoracolumbar spine xrays and DEXA. Clues to secondary causes may be ascertained from the above but frequently require selected laboratory studies for appropriate evaluation/diagnosis.

1. Assessment of risk factors is important in male and female patients from age 50 onward.
2. Preventive strategies of proper Calcium, Vitamin D, exercise and low risk lifestyle should be encouraged to try to maintain optimal health in all at risk populations.
3. Pharmacologic intervention should be strongly encouraged in those individuals with risk factors for fracture or multiple risk factors for decreased bone density.

HISTORY

Patient Demographics

▶ Age - pts over age 65 are known to be at higher risk for fracture

    ▸▸ Lower age does not exclude a diagnosis of osteoporosis

    ▸▸ Risk factor assessment is important - see below

▶ Gender - women have a higher risk for OP and fractures than men

    ▸▸ 1 in 4 women over the age of 50 have osteoporosis

    ▸▸ 1 in 8 men over the age of 50 have osteoporosis

▶ Ethnicity- Caucasians and Asians tend to be at higher risk than the black population

History of the Presenting Illness

Through the history, you should be able to determine risk factors for osteoporosis and the impact to date of the low bone density (Reference: CMAJ Nov 2002).

Ask about **"Risk Factors for Fracture"** as these highly correlated with increased risk of subsequent fracture

▶ **Age = 65**

▶ History of a previous **minimal trauma fracture**

    ▸▸ Also known as fragility or osteoporotic fracture

        ▸ Occurs with little or no trauma such as fall from standing height

    ▸▸ Most important are those fractures which occur after the age of 40

    ▸▸ Axial fractures

        ▸ May be difficult to pick up on history

            ◂ 1/3 present with sudden onset localized back pain,

            ◂ 2/3 are clinically silent initially

            ◂ history of height loss over time

    ▸▸ Peripheral fracture sites of concern include

        ▸ Wrist (Colle's fracture)

        ▸ Proximal humerus

        ▸ Hip

- ► Family history of Osteoporosis (see below)
- ► Low Bone Density (T score < - 2.5)
  - ▸ these last 2 are other risk factors for fracture but may be picked up in other places during your history

Other risk factors associated with osteoporosis/low bone density should be determined.

Lifestyle also influences the attainment of peak bone mass and subsequent maintenance of bone density. The following can be risk factors for osteoporosis

- ► Low calcium intake
- ► Smoker
- ► Excess alcohol intake
- ► Excess caffeine intake
- ► Inactivity

Secondary Causes of Bone Loss

Also, assessing the patient for secondary causes of bone loss can be accomplished in part through the history/functional inquiry.

- ► Hormonal insufficiency
  - ▸ Women - late menarche, early menopause, prolonged amenorrhea,
  - ▸ Men - testosterone deficiency
  - ▸ Consider disease and drugs which may interfere with normal hormonal function also (see below)
  - ▸ Malabsorption/malnutrition
- ► Inappropriately low body weight (hormonal and nutritional roles)
  - ▸ Loss of >10% of usual adult body weight
  - ▸ Inflammatory bowel disease (Crohn's and Ulcerative Colitis)
  - ▸ Celiac disease
  - ▸ Post GI surgery with significant resection
  - ▸ etc

- ► Selected other chronic illnesses
    - ⁍ Clinical hyperthyroidism
    - ⁍ Rheumatoid arthritis
    - ⁍ Disorders of mobility and balance

- ► Medication Use
    - ⁍ See below

History should also include: Previous investigations, Treatment to date, ADL.

Medication

Ask about medication(s) which can negatively affect bone density

- ► Glucocorticoids
    - ⁍ Greater than 3 months

- ► Anti-convulsant use (chronic)

- ► Heparin therapy (chronic)

- ► Also consider hormone suppressive medication
    - ⁍ E.g. Lupron, Arimidex

Ask about those which can positively affect bone mass

- ► Hormonal preparations
    - ⁍ Estrogens, testosterones etc

- ► Bisphosphonates

- ► Calcitonin

- ► Fluoride

Family History

Inquire about FHx of

- ► Osteoporotic fracture
    - ⁍ Fractures in either parent are relevant although maternal hip fracture carries the highest risk of low bone mass/fragility fracture

- ► Low bone mass
- ► Other illnesses as relevant

▶ Be on the look out for unusual histories which might suggest other metabolic bone diseases such as osteogenesis imperfecta

Past Medical History

Much of this may be covered in the HPI as many areas of health/illness can be pertinent to the osteoporosis history. Relevant other illnesses are too numerous to mention in detail. However, a few points may be helpful to remember.

Malignancy can affect the skeleton directly through the disease process, by the subsequent cachexia of malignancy and by some of the pharmacologic agents used to treat the underlying cancer. Most of this will be evident on the history/physical. Multiple myeloma can present as "osteoporosis" occasionally.

Renal disease is usually associated with other metabolic bone disease but osteoporosis can occur. When renal impairment is present, creatinine clearance is important to calculate when determining safe use of the bisphosphonates (cannot use with creatinine clearance <30 mL/s).

Impairment of sight is a risk factor for falling which can lead to an increased fracture risk. **Impairment of mobility and balance** carry similar risks. Falls cause fractures even when the bone density is normal but when increased risk of falling is combined with low bone density, the resultant risk of fragility fracture is markedly elevated.

PHYSICAL EXAMINATION

The general examination is helpful in ruling in/out secondary causes of decreased bone density.

The "specific" osteoporosis examination is axially based. Key points to assess and document:

▶ Height
  ▶▶ If previous height measurements are available - a loss of more than 2 cm is suggestive of a new vertebral fracture
  ▶▶ If "recalled" height is all that is available - a loss of 4 cm is likely significant
  ▶▶ Presence of a severe scoliosis or lower limb pathology decreases the usefulness of these guidelines

► Kyphosis

▸▸ "eyeball" this

▸▸ can be measured more precisely by a kyphometer but generally not done except in research

► Lateral lower rib to iliac crest distance

▸▸ Normal distance is 3 cm or greater

▸▸ This measurement decreases with lower thoracic and lumbar compression fracture

► Gait/balance

▸▸ Steady gait, good balance with standing and position change

▸▸ If poor, this increases risk of falling and subsequent fracture

KEY LABORATORY INVESTIGATION

Initial Investigations

► CBC

▸▸ general health status

▸▸ screening for nutritional status

▸▸▸ eg. Elevated MCV with folate deficiency in setting of malabsorption disease

► Calcium, Phosphate, Albumin

▸▸ Elevated calcium - think lab error (if only single sample)

▸▸▸ parathyroid disease, malignancy

▸▸▸ other causes - numerous but much less common

▸▸ Low Calcium - think chronic illness with low albumin

▸▸▸ Hypoparathyroidism (multiple causes)

▸▸▸ Vitamin D deficiency - dietary, Malabsorption diseases, Liver/renal disease

► Creatinine

▸▸ Elevated Cr - think other metabolic bone diseases

▸▸▸ monitor vitamin D status, may affect choice of pharmacologic agents

- ► Alkaline Phosphatase
    - ▸ Should be normal in osteoporosis
    - ▸ If elevated - think compression fracture, assess for lytic/osteo-clastic disease
    - ▸ If very low - assess for metabolic bone disease such as, hypophosphatasia
- ► Protein electrophoresis
    - ▸ If monoclonal gammopathy r/o multiple myeloma
- ► ESR
    - ▸ In older population to assess re multiple myeloma

Further Considerations

Assessment for **secondary causes of bone loss** is often prompted by the occurrence of a significant non-traumatic fracture history, a dramatic family history of fractures, abnormal screening lab work, or by the presence of unexpectedly low bone density of DEXA testing. *(If the Z score is < - 2.0, a diligent search for secondary causes of osteoporosis should be undertaken.)*

If clinical index of suspicion is high or the initial screening tests are abnormal consider:

- ► PTH (intact)
- ► Vitamin D (25 hydroxy Vit D or 1,25 dihydroxy Vitamin D)
- ► Creatinine clearance
- ► Immunoelectrophoresis
- ► 24 hour urine for Calcium excretion
- ► LH, FSH,
- ► Free or bioavailable testosterone levels
- ► TSH

IMAGING

Thoracolumbar spine lateral radiographs are very useful in assessing patients for vertebral fractures.

- ► Reminder: These fractures are the most frequent fractures in early post menopausal women and therefore clinically are very important.

▶ Significant loss of vertebral height = greater than 20% reduction in height when compared to a similar region of an adjacent vertebrae or when compared to the height of intact vertical regions of the same vertebra. (Anterior height loss often occurs first)

▶ It may take 3-6 weeks for compression to be visible on plain Xray.

Technetium Bone Scan should be considered if suspicious of new vertebral fracture and plain radiographs are unrevealing. Early fractures take time to reveal compression whereas the bone scan will usually be positive almost immediately after the fracture has occurred.

Dual Energy X-ray Absorptiometry (DEXA) is currently the best quantitative measure of bone mass and low levels of bone density as determined by this technology correlate well with increased occurrence of fragility fracture, especially in the older population. DEXA may also be useful in monitoring response to treatment over time.

World Health Organization Criteria for categorizing bone according to DEXA

▶ Normal: T score ranging from -1.0 to + 2.5 SD around the mean

▶ Osteopenia: T score -1.1 to -2.5 SD below the mean

▶ Osteoporosis: T score < -2.5 SD below the mean

Remember that the "mean" referred to by the T score is based on young, healthy adults and is sex matched.

Z scores may also be given in the DEXA data. Z scores compare bone mass to the individual's age matched controls/peer population. Low Z scores (Z score more than 2 SD below the age matched mean) suggest a higher probability of risk factors/secondary causes of low bone density. A diligent assessment for these risk factors/secondary causes should be undertaken.

TREATMENT OPTIONS

Non-Pharmacologic Intervention

▶ Encourage appropriate exercise

▶ Fall prevention strategies

▶ Hip protectors in suitable candidates

▶ Nutritional

⮕ Adequate Calcium intake (by diet or calcium supplementation)

- Calcium 1200-1500 mg / day in total
- Divided throughout the day
- Vitamin D supplementation (men and women)
  - Over age 50 - vitamin D_3 800 units/day
  - Under age 50 -   "400 units/day

Pharmacologic Measures

Review of the 2002 Clinical Practice Guidelines for the diagnosis and management of osteoporosis in Canada is strongly recommended for a summary of the current evidenced based recommendations.

Current drug therapies are limited to anti-resorptive agents.

Anti-Resorptive Agents

- Bisphosphonates (in order of "age" of drugs as they came to clinical use)
  - Etidronate
    - Best tolerated
    - Adequate effect for axial disease
    - Glucocorticoid induced osteoporosis (GIOP) can be minimized
    - No evidence to suggest reduction in peripheral fracture
    - Be careful in patients with significant renal disease

    Didrocal ® (Etidronate 400mg x 14 days q 12 weeks)

  - Alendronate and Risedronate
    - Excellent data to support fracture reduction in the osteoporotic patient - Axial and Peripheral (hip)
    - Specific protocol to minimize oesophageal irritation
    - Effective in minimizing GIOP and fractures
    - Appropriate for use in women and men
    - Contra-indicated in those with Creatinine Clearance < 30 ml/s

    Fosamax®   10 mg po od, 70 mg po q weekly
    Actonel®   5 mg po od,   35 mg po q weekly

As a class, these drugs are poorly absorbed and recommended dosing instructions must be followed for desired effectiveness. Adequate Calcium and vitamin D must be emphasized.

▶ Selective Estrogen Receptor Modulators
  ▸ Raloxifene
    ▹ Effective in reducing axial fractures in post menopausal women, No published hip data
    ▹ Causes hot flushes, Increases risk of venous thrombotic events, Cardiac effects appear benign but studies pending

    Evista® 60 mg po od

▶ Calcitonin
  ▸ Calcitonin Nasal Spray
    ▹ Second line treatment for osteoporosis
    ▹ Well tolerated usually
    ▹ No renal contraindications
    ▹ Does help minimize pain related to osteoporotic vertebral fractures
      ◂ Use in conjunction with analgesic therapy

    Miacalcin ® 200 units by nasal spray - alternate nostrils each day

▶ Hormone Replacement
  ▸ Estrogen
    ▹ Although estrogen has been shown to minimize osteoporotic fractures in post menopausal women, the side-effect profile is considerable and the use of estrogen is not recommended as a first line agent for the management of osteoporosis.
  ▸ Testosterone
    ▹ In the male population, the use of testosterone may be helpful in those instances where testosterone deficiency has been documented clearly. Routine use in the management of male osteoporosis does not appear warranted at the present time.

PEARLS

1. In the adult population, all fragility fractures carry with them an increased risk of subsequent fragility fracture and investigation and treatment are to be strongly considered.

2. All patients starting glucocorticoid therapy must be considered at high risk for osteoporosis and its consequences - specifically vertebral fracture. This can occur within the first year of steroid therapy particularly in high dose steroids or in those already at risk for osteoporosis/fractures.

   Suitable treatment is required. At the very least, consider:

   a. Calcium and vitamin D intake should be optimized

   b. Counseling regarding suitable life style habits (tobacco avoidance, minimal alcohol and caffeine, exercise as able etc)

   c. DEXA testing as baseline

   d. DEXA testing 6-12 months after institution of corticosteroids depending on patient's other risk factors, level of health (or lack thereof) and steroid dose

   Use of a bisphosphonate can be helpful as preventative or therapeutic strategy.

3. Z scores of < - 2.0 indicate that bone density is unexpectedly low for an individual's age and as such, suitable investigation is required.

REFERENCES

1. CMAJ 2002; 167 (10 suppl): S1-S34, 2002 Clinical Practice Guidelines for the Diagnosis and Management of Osteoporosis in Canada

2. JAMA 2002; 288: 321-333 Writing Group for the Women's Health Initiative

[Section 3]

Approach to Selection and Interpretation of Laboratory Tests in Rheumatic Diseases

[9] Approach to Selection and Interpretation of Laboratory Tests

Dr. Kam Shojania, University of British Columbia

PRACTICAL USE OF LABORATORY TESTS IN RHEUMATOLOGY

KEY CONCEPTS

There are 3 reasons to order a laboratory test in rheumatology:

1. To confirm a diagnosis or determine extent of a disease (e.g. ANA in systemic lupus erythematosus)
2. To monitor disease activity (e.g. ESR in giant cell arteritis)
3. To monitor drug toxicity (e.g. Transaminase monitoring when using methotrexate)

Laboratory tests are useful only as an adjunct to a thorough history and physical examination and can only be interpreted within a specific clinical situation. A good clinician will be wary of putting too much emphasis on the laboratory. In general, a diagnostic test is most helpful when the sensitivity and specificity are high, and the pretest probability of a positive test is around 50%.

INTRODUCTION

To determine the usefulness of test in a specific situation, one needs to know two things:

1. The intrinsic qualities of the test (these are constant)
    A. Sensitivity: The proportion of patients with the disease that have a positive test.
    B. Specificity: The proportion of patients without the disease that have a negative test.
2. The likelihood of the disease in a particular situation (pre-test probability) which is obtained by doing a thorough history and physical examination.

Pretest probability: The clinician estimates the likelihood of the disease before the test is performed.

Posttest probability: Using Bayes theorem one can calculate the posttest probability using the following equation:

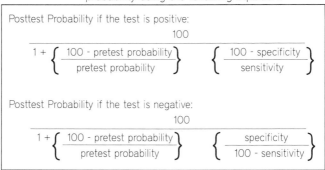

Let us use the example of HLA-B27. In a Caucasian patient, the sensitivity is 92% and the specificity is 92% for ankylosing spondylitis. After examining the patient, you decide that your pretest probability that the patient has ankylosing spondylitis is 50%. Application of Bayes theorem will result in the following post-test probabilities:

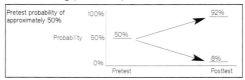

So with a pretest probability of 50% the HLA B27 test is quite helpful if it is positive or negative. However, if your pretest probability of ankylosing spondylitis is very low or very high, the test becomes less helpful. The following graph represents the outcomes of using the HLA B27 test in 2 patients, one with a low pretest probability (10%) and another with a high pretest probability (90%):

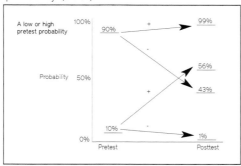

The 50:50 rule:

If your pre-test likelihood of a test is about 50%,

► The posttest likelihood that a patient <u>has</u> the disease given a <u>positive</u> test approximately = <u>specificity</u>.
► The posttest likelihood that a patient <u>doesn't have</u> the disease given a <u>negative</u> test approximately = <u>sensitivity</u>.

The remainder of this chapter will review the benefits of specific laboratory tests used in rheumatology:

Section I	Section II
ESR and CRP Rheumatoid factor ANA ENA Anti-DNA Complement ANCA Uric acid	Synovial fluid analysis

SECTION I. SEROLOGY TESTING

Erythrocyte sedimentation rate (ESR) and C-reactive protein (CRP)

Description of test

The ESR is a measure of the rate at which red blood cells settle through a column of liquid. Measuring the ESR takes approximately 1 hour and is relatively inexpensive compared with the C-reactive protein test. C-reactive protein is produced by the liver during periods of inflammation and is detectable in the blood serum of patients with various infectious or inflammatory diseases.

Use

These are nonspecific tests that are sometimes helpful in distinguishing between inflammatory and noninflammatory conditions. However, they are not diagnostic and may be abnormal in a vast array of infectious, malignant, rheumatic and other diseases.

An ESR above 40 mm/h may indicate polymyalgia rheumatica or giant cell arteritis if the patient's history and physical examination are compatible with either diagnosis. Unfortunately, the ESR may be below 40 mm/h in up to 20% of patients with these conditions. A very high CRP or ESR (>100) should prompt consideration of vasculitis, significant infection or malignancy.

The ESR may be useful for monitoring patients with rheumatoid arthritis, polymyalgia rheumatica and giant cell arteritis, where a rise in ESR may herald a worsening of the disease when a corticosteroid dose is being tapered. This should not automatically result in an increase in the corticosteroid dose, but rather closer observation and perhaps a more gradual tapering of the corticosteroid.

Common Pitfalls

Using the ESR to screen for inflammation is usually not helpful because the rate can rise with anemia, infections and the use of certain medications such as cholesterol-lowering drugs. The ESR will also rise with age and is of extremely limited value in the elderly; an elevated ESR in an elderly patient should not prompt further investigation in the absence of clinical findings. A rough rule of thumb for the upper limit for ESR with increasing age is age/2 in men and (age+10)/2 in women. The C-reactive protein test is slightly more reliable than the ESR and does not rise with anemia.

Rheumatoid Factor (RF)

Description of Test

"Rheumatoid factor" is a misnomer; it confers a specificity to this test that is not deserved. Rheumatoid factors are immunoglobulin M antibodies directed against the Fc (constant) region of the immunoglobulin G molecule. Their presence can be detected with a wide variety of techniques (e.g., agglutination of sheep red blood cells, latex particles coated with human immunoglobulin G, enzyme-linked immunosorbent assay or nephelometry). Unfortunately, the measurement is not standardized in many laboratories. Rheumatoid factor is present in most people at very low levels, but higher levels are present in 5%-10% of the population, and this percentage rises with age.

Use

Many conditions can cause an elevated rheumatoid factor (Table 1). Only 60% of patients with rheumatoid arthritis test positive for rheumatoid factor. However, in patients with rheumatoid arthritis a high-titre test (= 1:512) may predict a more severe disease course. This test should be done only if a patient shows evidence of polyarticular joint inflammation for more than 6 weeks. Serial testing is not useful for patients with rheumatoid arthritis or any other condition.

Table 1. Some conditions associated with a positive rheumatoid factor

Rheumatologic diseases	Other conditions
Rheumatoid arthritis Sjogren's syndrome Scleroderma Polymyositis/dermatomyositis Mixed connective tissue disease Sarcoidosis Systemic lupus erythematosus	Cryoglobulinemia Endocarditis Mycobacterial diseases Viral hepatitis Syphilis Old age

Common Pitfalls

This is not useful as a screening test. It is nonspecific and insensitive: the presence of rheumatoid factor does not indicate rheumatoid arthritis, nor does its absence rule out rheumatoid arthritis. A positive RF in a patient with nonspecific symptoms may precipitate unnecessary investigations.

Test for antinuclear antibodies

Description

Antinuclear antibodies (ANAs) are diverse. Some have specific disease associations. A positive ANA is 1 of 11 criteria used in the diagnosis SLE. This is a useful screening test if SLE is suspected, as a negative test virtually rules out SLE. Many autoimmune diseases are associated with a positive ANA test. The ANA test is positive in 98% of patients with SLE, 40-70% of those with other connective tissue diseases, up to 20% with autoimmune thyroid and liver disease and in 5% of healthy adults (at a cut-off titre of 1:160).

Table 2. Some conditions associated with a positive ANA

Rheumatologic Disease	Other conditions
SLE MCTD Scleroderma Sjögren's	Autoimmune liver disease (autoimmune hepatitis, primary biliary cirrhosis) Autoimmune thyroid disease Healthy relatives of SLE patients Neoplasia Old age

Results are reported as a titre with a pattern (Table 3), which is occasionally useful in making a diagnosis of a connective tissue disease.

Table 3. Common patterns of antinuclear antibodies

Pattern	Association	Further tests suggested
Speckled	Non-specific	Test for extractable nuclear antigens may be helpful
Homogeneous	Non-specific	None
Nucleolar	Diffuse scleroderma	Test for anti-topoisomerase antibodies may be helpful
Centromere	Limited scleroderma (CREST)	None
Rim	SLE (Anti-dsDNA)	Check anti-dsDNA

CREST = Calcinosis, Raynaud's phenomenon, Esophageal dysmotility, Sclerodactyly, Telangiectasias;
dsDNA = double-stranded deoxyribonucleic acid;
SLE = systemic lupus erythematosus

Use

An ANA should be ordered when a connective tissue disease such as SLE is suspected based on several specific findings on history or physical examination. These findings could include photosensitivity, malar rash, alopecia, mouth ulcers, sicca symptoms, Raynaud's phenomenon, inflammatory arthritis or pleuropericarditis. If the test is negative, SLE can usually be ruled out. However, a positive test does not by itself ensure a diagnosis of a connective tissue disease. Serial testing is of no value as it does not accurately monitor disease activity.

Common pitfalls

At a cut-off titre of 1:40, a staggering 32% of the normal population are positive for ANAs (13% are positive at a titre of 1:80). In that only 0.1% of the population have SLE, a low-titre ANA is almost always of no consequence. If history and physical examination are unremarkable, no further investigation of a positive ANA should be done.

Tests for antibodies to extractable nuclear antigens

Description

Extractable nuclear antigens (ENAs) are specific antinuclear antibodies obtained from the blood. There are a large number of ENAs, but most are used for research purposes. ENAs that are commercially available include anti-La, anti-Smith, anti-RNP and in some labs, anti-Ro and anti-Jo.

Use

A test for antibodies to extractable nuclear antigens (anti-ENA) should be ordered only if there is a suspected or known connective tissue disease and the ANA test is positive at a significant titre (1:160 or higher). Many of the anti-ENA tests are helpful if positive (Table 4), and some indicate the possibility of more severe disease manifestations. For example, the presence of anti-Jo antibodies in dermatomyositis often predicts an aggressive course of the disease with interstitial lung disease and inflammatory arthritis.

Table 4. Rheumatic diseases associated with extractable nuclear antigens

Extractable nuclear antigen	Rheumatic disease associations
anti-Sm	Highly specific for SLE but low sensitivity
anti-Ro (SSA)	Occurs in SLE especially with cutaneous involvment and is common in Sjögrens. Antibodies in the mother makes neonatal SLE, including congenital heart block, more likely
anti-La (SSB)	Sjögrens syndrome, SLE
anti-RNP	Nonspecific but is part of the criteria for MCTD. Also occurs in SLE
anti-Jo-1	Highly specific for a severe form of PM/DM but not sensitive
anti-histone	Seen in SLE and drug-induced SLE
anticentromere	Often found in limited scleroderma (CREST)
anti-topoisomerase (Scl-70)	Sometimes found in diffuse scleroderma, can correlate with interstitial lung disease in scleroderma.

Common pitfalls

There are no major pitfalls, although the test is rarely needed and it would rarely be ordered by the primary care physician. As most anti-ENA tests have low sensitivity, negative tests are usually not helpful. An exception would be a negative anti-Ro or anti-La in a pregnant patient with SLE, which may predict a smaller chance of having a child with neonatal lupus.

Test for antibodies to double-stranded DNA (anti-dsDNA)

Description

Antibodies to DNA can be divided into 2 groups: those that react to denatured or single-stranded DNA (ssDNA) and those recognizing double-stranded DNA (dsDNA). Tests for anti-ssDNA have limited usefulness and are not generally available. In contrast, anti-dsDNA antibodies are relatively specific (95%) for SLE, making them useful for diagnosis. However, although a negative test does not rule out the disease as they occur only in up to 30% of patients with SLE.

Use

This test should be ordered only when SLE is suspected after history or physical examination have been carried out and when an ANA test is positive. The presence of anti-dsDNA may predict a more severe form of SLE with renal or central nervous system involvement. Some clinicians suggest that this test may be useful in following the clinical course of SLE, although this is disputed. Most rheumatologists would not treat an isolated rise in anti-dsDNA level in the absence of a clinical flare. The anti-dsDNA test is one of the 11 diagnostic criteria for SLE.

Common pitfalls

This test should never be performed as part of a routine screening process for patients with aches and pains.

Complement C3 and C4

Description

Decreased levels of complement arise from immune complex disorders such as SLE, selected forms of vasculitis (e.g., essential mixed cryoglobulinemia and rheumatoid vasculitis), certain types of glomerulonephritis and as an inherited disorder.

Use

They are useless as screening tests. Complement testing is often used to monitor disease activity in patients with SLE, but the evidence for this is sparse. It is expected that an SLE flare will result in decreased complement levels. An elevated complement level is a nonspecific finding with no clinical relevance.

Table 5. Some causes of Low Serum Complements

Rheumatic Disease	Other Diseases
Systemic Lupus Erythematosus (may have hereditary complement deficiencies) Cryoglobulinemia Rheumatoid Vasculitis Systemic vasculitis (especially PAN and urticarial vasculitis)	Subacute bacterial endocarditis Bacterial sepsis Viremias Parasitemias

Common pitfalls

In some patients with known vasculitis or SLE, complement levels may reflect disease activity. Ten to 15% of Caucasian patients with SLE will have an inherited complement deficiency. Repeated testing of these people is not helpful.

Antineutrophil cytoplasmic antibody test

Description

ANCAs are autoantibodies to the cytoplasmic constituents of granulocytes. They are detected by indirect immunofluorescence on ethanol-fixed neutrophils and produce a characteristic cytoplasmic fluorescence (c-ANCA) or perinuclear fluorescence (p-ANCA). ANCAs characteristically occur in vasculitic syndromes. In vasculitis, the relevant target antigens are proteinase 3 (PR3) for c-ANCA and myeloperoxidase (MPO) for p-ANCA.

ANCAs occur in more than 90% of patients with systemic Wegener's granulomatosis (with renal and/or pulmonary involvement), 75% of patients with limited Wegener's granulomatosis (without renal involvement) and 50% of patients with microscopic polyangiitis. The presence of PR3-ANCA is 98% specific for these diseases. However, note that the absence of ANCA does not exclude the diagnosis of Wegener's Granulomatosis. In patients positive for c-ANCA, changes in the level may reflect disease activity but cannot be used reliably to guide treatment.

p-ANCAs occur in a wide range of diseases. They are directed against different cytoplasmic constituents of neutrophils, including myeloperoxidase, lactoferrin, elastase and other unspecified antigens. Therefore, a positive p-ANCA is nonspecific. Only antibodies to myeloperoxidase (MPO) have significant vasculitis associations. A small percentage of Wegener's patients are MPO-ANCA positive. Approximately 70% of patients with microscopic polyangiitis are MPO-ANCA positive. MPO-ANCA may also be seen in Churg-Strauss vasculitis.

Use

The c-ANCA test can be helpful in confirming a diagnosis of Wegener's granulomatosis, microscopic polyangiitis or idiopathic crescentic glomerulonephritis. PR3-ANCA has a high specificity of 98% for these conditions. It has a high sensitivity for systemic Wegener's granulomatosis (with renal involvement), but less sensitive for the limited condition (without renal involvement). A positive c-ANCA test in a patient with typical Wegener's granulomatosis may obviate the need for a tissue biopsy. The p-ANCA test is not useful unless it is confirmed by testing for anti-myeloperoxidase antibodies (anti-MPO) which may occur in several related diseases: Churg Strauss syndrome, crescentic glomerulonephritis and microscopic polyangiitis.

Common pitfalls

This test helps in the diagnosis and management of only a very small number of patients with relatively rare conditions. A primary care physician will rarely need to order this test. Using ANCA to screen patients with non-specific symptoms results in many false positive p-ANCA tests. Immunofluorescence produces p- ANCA's in patients with immune-mediated conditions such as collagen vascular disease, inflammatory bowel disease and autoimmune hepatitis. However, these are not true MPO-ANCA's and may have other antigen specificities as outlined above.

Serum uric acid test

Use

This test is helpful in monitoring the extent of hyperuricemia in patients with gout requiring treatment. The prevalence of asymptomatic hyperuricemia among men is 5%-8%, and fewer than 1 in 3 people with hyperuricemia will ever develop gout. Asymptomatic hyperuricemia does not confer a diagnosis of gout and need not be treated unless serum uric acid levels are persistently above 760 μmol/L (12.8 mg/dL) for men or 600 μmol/L (10.0 mg/dL) for women. At these levels there is an increased risk of renal complications.

Common pitfalls

Uric acid testing is often ordered for the patient with acute monoarthritis. Unfortunately, this will not be helpful in the diagnosis because of the high prevalence of asymptomatic hyperuricemia and the fact that, in 10% of patients with acute gout, serum uric acid levels are normal. A diagnosis of acute gout can only be made with certainty by joint aspiration to confirm the presence of urate crystals under polarized light.

Section II. Synovial Fluid Testing

Description

Synovial fluid, obtained by joint aspiration, is examined visually for viscosity and tested for cell count and differential, gram staining, bacteria and the presence of crystals under polarized light (Table 6).

Table 6. Characteristics of synovial fluid in specific diseases

	Normal	Non-inflammatory	Rheumatoid arthritis	Gout or pseudogout	Septic arthritis	Hemorrhagic
Colour	Transparent	Transparent	Translucent/opaque	Translucent/opaque	Opaque	Bloody
Viscosity	High	High	Low	Low	Variable	Variable
Gram stain	Negative	Negative	Negative	Negative	Positive	Negative
Bacterial culture	Negative	Negative	Negative	Negative	Positive	Negative
Cell count x 10^9 L	<200	200-2,000	2000-10,000	2000-40,000	>50,000	200-2000
% PMNLs	<25	<25	>50	>50	>75	50-75
Crystals	Negative	Negative	Negative	Positive	Negative	Negative

PMNL = polymorphonuclear leukocyte

The assessment of polymorphonuclear leukocytes is essential in the investigation of an acute inflammatory monoarthritis to diagnose septic arthritis or crystal joint disease. A white blood cell count of less than 2000 x10^9/L indicates a non-inflammatory effusion. Inflammatory effusions are often accompanied by a white blood cell count of 2000-50 000 x10^9/L and infectious arthritis usually occurs with white blood cell counts over 50 000 X10^9/L, with a predominance of neutrophils. Other tests of value in specific clinical situations are mycobacteria tuberculosis staining and culture, fungal culture or cytological examination.

Ideally, examination for crystals should be carried out using a fresh sample of synovial fluid. To find calcium pyrophosphate dihydrate crystals, a fresh specimen is essential. If the attending physician is unable to examine the fresh specimen, the laboratory must be alerted to the fact that a fresh specimen must be reviewed urgently. Intracellular crystals are the most specific. Monosodium urate crystals, seen with gout, are needle shaped and strongly negatively birefringent. The calcium pyrophosphate dihidrate crystals of pseudogout are weakly positively birefringent and rhomboid in shape.

Common pitfalls

The most common pitfalls occur when this test is not done. Synovial fluid testing must be done to make a diagnosis of infectious or crystal synovitis. Chemistry testing (glucose, lactic dehydrogenase, protein) of synovial fluid is not helpful in making such a diagnosis.

REFERENCES

Standard references listed in introduction.

[10] Approach to the Interpretation of Musculoskeletal Imaging

Dr. Volodko Bakowsky, Dalhousie University

KEY CONCEPTS

▶ Imaging studies need to be guided by a thorough history and physical examination. Interpreting radiologic investigations in isolation can be misleading because: 1. the real pathology can be at a site distant to where the symptoms are, eg posterior thigh pain may be referred from the spine and 2. radiographic findings may not always correlate well with symptoms, eg minor degenerative changes on Xray may be asymptomatic.

▶ It is important to understand the relative utility of various imaging modalities in order to select the most appropriate test

▶ Plain film radiography is usually the first modality used, as it is readily available and inexpensive

▶ Always use a structured approach to interpreting joint Xrays. This allows you to evaluate the study thoroughly in an organized fashion.

▶ Try to anticipate the radiographic findings before you see them, based on information you obtained in your history and physical exam.

PLAIN FILM RADIOGRAPHY

The imaging study initially selected is almost always plain film radiography. Plain films offer excellent resolution of bony structures, but are very poor at evaluating soft tissue structures. In fact, most non-bony structures such as cartilage, muscle, tendons and synovial fluid all appear to have the same radiodensity. Cartilage destruction has to be inferred by narrowing of the joint space. Plain films are widely available and low in cost.

When peripheral joints are evaluated, the patient is exposed to low radiation doses. Spinal and pelvic radiographs require exposure to higher radiation doses and should be selected with greater care, especially in younger patients.

As plain films of joints are 2D images of 3D structures, usually more than one profile is required.

Hands: For evaluation of arthritis, often a PA view and ball-catcher's view are adequate. If looking for traumatic changes, a lateral is also required. The PA view highlights the DIP, PIP, MCP joints and the carpus. The ball-catchers view profiles the triquetrum and pisiform and radial aspect of MCP joints where early changes can occur in RA. In this position, the hands are not held in a fixed position therefore reducible subluxations (as in Jaccoud's arthropathy) can be visualized. Plain Xrays of the hands are often quite useful in the evaluation of inflammatory arthritis, as changes occur relatively early here due to the fact that the articular cartilage is relatively thin compared to larger joints (a principle that also applies to the feet).

Feet: AP, oblique and lateral views are usually obtained. The AP view highlights the IP, MTP and first and second MTT joints. The oblique view allows visualization of the 3rd to 5th MTT joint. The lateral view profiles the calcaneus, subtalar joint, the dorsal aspect of the MTT joints and the insertions of the plantar fascia and Achilles tendons.

Shoulder: The 40 degree posterior oblique view allows profiling of the glenohumeral joint. A standard AP view does not, but better profiles the AC joint. Both visualize the subacromial space. Y views are usually also obtained routinely. This view produces the "Mercedes Benz sign" where the head of the humerus is centred on the spine of the scapula and proximal humerus and bears a striking resemblance to this famous hood ornament. This sign indicates that the shoulder has not suffered an anterior dislocation.

Elbow: Standard views include an AP and lateral view.

Hip: Standard views include an AP of the pelvis and frogleg lateral positions.

Knee: Standard views include a standing AP (considerable joint space narrowing may be missed by a non-weight bearing view), and semi-flexed lateral view. The latter view allows evaluation of the patello-femoral joint to some degree, although dedicated skyline views should be obtained for optimal visualization of these joints.

Spine: Standard views include AP and lateral. Specialized views can include obliques of the C-spine to look for intervertebral foraminal encroachment, flexion and extension views of the C spine to look for C1-C2 subluxation and obliques of the lumbar spine to look for spondylolysis.

SI Joints: These might be seen in a standard AP of the lumbar spine, but to profile the SI joints specifically, HIBs or Ferguson's views are often necessary. In this view, the Xray tube is angled 25-30° in a cephalad direction. Remember, the area one is most interested in is the inferior 1/3 of the joint as this is the synovial portion of the SI joint. Pathology of the SI joints is usually demonstrated on the iliac side of the joint first as this side has thinner cartilage.

APPROACH TO EVALUATING A RADIOGRAPH OF A JOINT

A systematic and organized approach is helpful when interpreting radiographs. The mnemonic *Sometimes Bad Nosebleeds Can't Just Stop Ever Dripping Down* is useful to remember the essential aspects one should remember to evaluate.

Some Times (Soft Tissue)
BaD (Bone Density)
Nose Bleeds (New Bone Formation)
Can't (Calcification)
Just Stop (Joint Space)
Ever (Erosions)
Dripping (Deformity)
Down (Distribution)

Soft Tissue: Remember, plain films are not terribly good at identifying abnormalities in soft tissue. You may, however, be able to see soft tissue swelling surrounding swollen joints. In inflammatory arthritis this is usually symmetrical around the joint. Asymmetrical swelling can occur when there are underlying osteophytes or tophi. Swelling of an entire digit, otherwise known as a sausage digit, is relatively specific for a seronegative spondyloarthritis such as reactive arthritis or psoriatic arthritis.

Bone Density: Bone density is usually a subjective assessment and radiographic technique can influence how osteopenic the bones can look. Juxta-articular osteopenia means diminished bone density in the bone surrounding a joint. It can be one of the earliest findings in an inflammatory arthritis, however, it is often too subjective to be used reliably and can lack specificity when interpreted by non-experts. In the hand, the sum of the two cortices of the shaft of the second or third metacarpal should equal at least one half its width in a normal digit. If this is not the case, generalized osteopenia can be said to be present. This can occur in RA and in osteoporosis. Maintenance of normal bone density can be a feature of a seronegative spondyloarthritis.

New Bone Formation: New bone can form in a variety of settings. In OA, new bone is formed at the joint margins of affected joints. This type of new bone is called an osteophyte. New bone can also form underneath the articular cartilage in OA. This produces whiter, more radiodense bone and is known as subchondral sclerosis. An enthesophyte is new bone formation at sites of tendinous or ligamentous insertion into bone. This can be a degenerative process, eg a heel spur, or a manifestation of a seronegative spondyloarthritis. The articular margin of a degenerative enthesophyte is quite clear, whereas an enthesophyte secondary to a seronegative spondyloarthritis has margins that are somewhat indistinct, and it is sometimes accompanied by an erosion in the adjacent bony cortex. Periosteal new bone formation in the phalanges is another sign of a seronegative spondyloarthritis. This can have a "whiskered" appearance. New bone can even grow right across the joint line causing fusion or ankylosis. OA can cause fusion of DIP and PIP joints. RA does not cause fusion beyond the wrist or the ankle. Seronegative sponyloarthropathies can cause fusion distal to the wrist and ankle, and they are also capable of causing fusion of the spine and SI joints.

Calcification: Calcification is different than new bone formation or ossification. The margins of the area of calcification are very indistinct, and the radiodensity is lower than that of new bone. CPPD deposits may calcify. This may occur in areas of fibrocartilage, eg menisci, triangular fibro-cartilage of the wrist or symphysis pubis, or in hyaline cartilage. Calcification of cartilage is also known as chondrocalcinosis. Calcification of para-articular tendons, eg supraspinatus tendon can also occur and is usually post-traumatic or due to hydroxyapatite deposition disease. Calcification of gouty tophi may also occur.

Joint Space: Uniform joint space narrowing affects all areas of the joint equally and is typically found in an inflammatory arthritis. Non-uniform joint space narrowing is said to be present when certain regions of the joint are affected to a greater degree and is usually a feature of OA. For example, OA of the knee often affects the medial compartment predom-inantly. In gout, the joint space is often maintained until very late in the disease process.

Erosions: In RA and seronegative spondyloarthritis, the inflammatory reaction can result in erosion of the bony cortex near the joint margin. This location is known as the "bare area" as there is no overlying articu-lar cartilage, thus exposing the bone to inflammatory change much ear-lier than the bone that is protected by a cartilage cap. On a PA view, these type of erosions can look like "mouse ears". In seronegative spondyloarthritis, erosions can cause the bone surrounding the joint to appear whittled away, the so called "pencil in a cup" erosive change. In OA of the DIP and PIP joints, central erosions can appear which cause the joint line to appear like a seagull in profile. When these changes are present, they are often described as representing "erosive OA". This is a radiographic term that is sometimes confusing. Just remember that there is no difference between erosive OA and non-erosive OA other than how it looks on Xray. Also note, OA does not cause erosive change any-where else. In gout, tophi very slowly expand into the bone cortex, allow-ing the bone to remodel and try to repair itself. This results in "chronic ero-sions" where you can visualize overhanging cortex surrounding the erosion.

Deformity: One must note the presence of joint subluxation, and in its severest form, dislocation. RA has many famous deformities associated with it such as ulnar deviation of the digits at the MCP joints, swan neck and boutonniere deformities. These can also occur in seronegative spondyloarthropathies.

Distribution: At the end, one should summarize the findings you have already noted, plus provide commentary on the distribution of changes. **OA** tends to affect DIP, PIP, first CMC and first MTP joints as well as the hips, knees, AC joints, C Spine and L Spine. **RA** can affect virtually all the joints, but tends to spare the DIP joints and spine other than the C spine. **Seronegative spondyloarthropathies** can be oligoarticular and asymmetrical and can involve the spine, SI joints and DIP joints. Sometimes an entire ray is affected, eg the MCP, PIP and DIP joint of the same finger. Other times, the distribution can mimic that of RA. **Gout** tends to more commonly affect the lower extremities.

OTHER IMAGING MODALITIES

Arthrography

Radiocontrast can be administered under fluoroscopic guidance into the shoulder or wrist. One can then evaluate the shoulder for full thickness rotator cuff tears and the wrist for tears of the triangular fibrocartilage or carpal ligaments.

Bone scan

Images from bone scans are typically performed in 3 phases. The first phase or flow phase is a marker of blood flow to a region, which can be increased for a variety of reasons. The next phase is called "blood pool" and can show abnormal radiopharmaceutical uptake due to both bony and soft tissue disease. The delayed phase is most important for evaluation of bony structures and is obtained several hours after the injection of the radiopharmaceutical. By this time, most uptake due to soft tissue problems such as cellulitis should have dissipated. Bone scan is a very sensitive technique which can demonstrate areas of early osteomyelitis, stress fractures, avascular necrosis and metastatic disease much earlier than plain films. It can also identify diseased joints as the para-articular bone often lights up on the scan. The resolution on born scans is only fair, which limits its usefulness in diagnosis. The cost is about the same for a CT scan.

CT scan

CT scanning provides much better soft tissue contrast than plain films. It can demonstrate bony changes earlier than plain films in osteomyelitis or avascular necrosis.

It is also of great help evaluating the cross-sectional anatomy of structures that are too complex to be well visualized with plain films, eg hindfoot, SI joints and sternoclavicular joints. It is often readily available and is less expensive than MRI. CT scan can also be performed after intraarticular contrast is administered.

MRI

MRI scanning is the best modality for evaluating soft tissue. It derives structural information from the density of protons which differ in various types of tissue. The strength and timing of magnetic field pulses are changed to produce different types of images with differing characteristics. A full explanation of MRI is beyond the scope of this chapter but there are some basic rules which can help you with interpretation of MR images. Normal fatty bone marrow is bright on T1, and slightly less bright on T2 images. Pathologic processes (infiltrative disease, infection, and bone marrow edema) will be low signal on a T1 study. Synovial fluid, edema, and cysts are bright on T2 images. Fat suppressed techniques such as STIR, illustrate bone marrow edema better by reducing the signal returned from fatty tissue such as bone marrow compared to T2 images. Indications for MRI include internal derangement of the knee, avascular necrosis (most sensitive modality for this diagnosis), rotator cuff tears, early sacroiliitis, evaluation of soft tissue tumours and to look for neurologic impingement at the level of the spine. MRI can be performed either after intraarticular or intravenous gadolinium is administered. The former technique can help diagnose subtle abnormalities such as labral tears of the shoulder and hip. The latter technique can identify synovial proliferation from an inflammatory arthritis.

Ultrasound

Ultrasound is helpful in confirming Baker's cysts and evaluating the integrity of the rotator cuff and Achilles tendons.

SUMMARY OF THE RADIOGRAPHIC FINDINGS IN COMMON RHEUMATIC DISEASES

Disease	Soft Tissue Swelling	Bone Density	New Bone Formation	Calcification
Osteoarthritis	+/- asymmetrical	Normal	Osteophytes, subchondral sclerosis	No
Rheumatoid Arthritis	+/- symmetrical	Normal or ↓	Generally no, may have fusion of wrist and ankles	No
Seronegative Spondyloarthritis	+/- symmetrical, may have sausage digit	Normal or ↑	Periosteal new bone formation, may have fusion distal to wrist and ankles, and in spine. Also ossification at entheses	No
Gout	+/- asymmetrical	N	No	Occasionally
CPPD	+/- symmetrical	N	No	Often

Joint Space	Erosions	Deformity	Distribution
Often non-uniform	Generally no, but may have central erosions in DIPs and PIPs of hands	+	DIP, PIP, first CMC, AC, hip, knee, first MTP, lumbar and cervical spine
Uniform	Marginal erosions	+++	Spares DIP joints and axial skeleton other than cervical spine
Uniform	Marginal erosions	++	May be asymmetrical and oligoarticular or occasionally RA pattern. SI joints and entire spine can be involved. Entheses can also be involved
Not until very late	Chronic erosions with overhanging edge	+	Often lower extremity predominance
Uniform or non-uniform	NO	+	CPPD most commonly occurs in shoulder, elbows, wrists, MCP, and knees. Chondrocalcinosis most commonly noted at wrists, knees, and symphysis pubis

EXAMPLES OF HAND RADIOGRAPHS IN VARIOUS ARTHROPATHIES

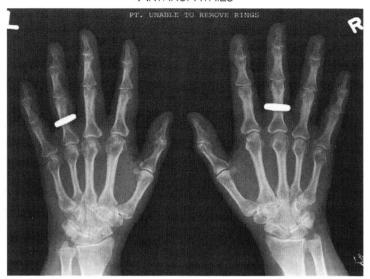

There is no soft tissue swelling. Bone density is normal. There is new bone production at several DIP joints (osteophytes). There is no calcification. There is joint space narrowing at multiple DIP joints, most notable at DIP #3 on the right and #3 and 4 on the left. There is a central erosion present at the left 4th DIP joint. There is no deformity. This is osteoarthritis of the DIP joints.

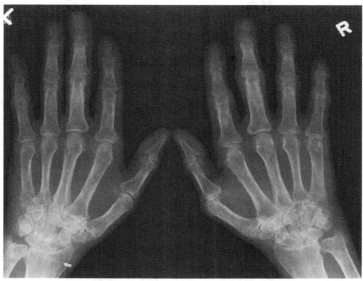

There is symmetrical soft tissue swelling around PIP joint 3 and 5 on the right. There is generalized osteopenia. There is no new bone formation or calcification. There is narrowing of multiple PIP and MCP joints and in both radiocarpal joints. There are erosions present at the 2nd MCP joints and the left second PIP joint. There is subluxation of the right fifth middle phalanx on the proximal phalanx. These are hands of a patient with RA.

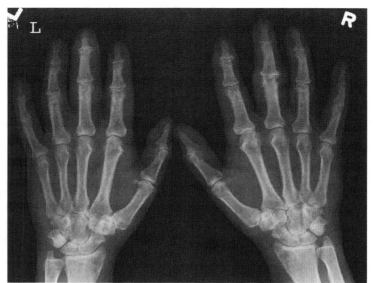

There is soft tissue swelling that looks symmetrical around the right third PIP joint. There is new bone formation at the left third and right second DIP joints and at the middle phalangeal margin of the right third PIP joint (osteophytes). There is sclerosis at the left first CMC joint (subchondral sclerosis). There is no calcification. The Right third PIP joint and second DIP joint spaces are mildly narrowed and there is marked narrowing of the left third DIP joint. There is a large chronic erosion with overhanging cortical margin at the right third PIP joint. There is no deformity present. This is a patient with gout of his right 3rd PIP joint. The OA changes at his left third and right second DIP joints and at the base of his left thumb are incidental findings.

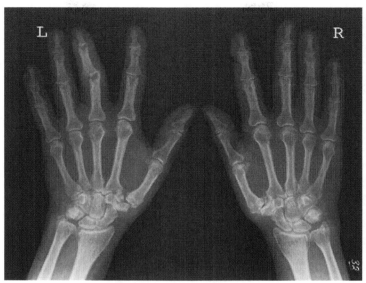

There is soft tissue swelling of the entire left third digit. Bone density is maintained. There is new bone formation at the base of the distal phalanx of the left third finger. There is no calcification. The joint space of the left third DIP and PIP joints is narrowed. There are large erosions present at these joints as well. There is ulnar subluxation of the left third phalanx at the PIP joint. This is an example of a seronegative spondyloarthritis affecting an entire ray. Incidental note is made of a bone fragment at the ulnar styloid from previous trauma and OA changes at the first CMC joint of the right thumb.

REFERENCES

1. Evaluation of the Patient F. Imaging Techniques. In: Klippel J, Crofford L, Stone J, Weyand C, eds. Primer on the Rheumatic Diseases. 12th ed. Atlanta: The Arthritis Foundation; 2001. p146-156.

2. Brower A. Arthritis is Black and White. 2nd ed. W.B. Saunders, 1997.

[Section 4]
Approach to Therapeutics

[11] Pharmacologic Agents

Dr. Lori Albert, University of Toronto

KEY CONCEPTS

▶ Some therapeutic agents, such as NSAIDS, can be used to manage mild and non-specific symptoms. However, the use of corticosteroids and other immunosuppressive agents should only be undertaken after every effort has been made to clarify the diagnosis.

▶ While it is advisable to avoid polypharmacy as much as possible, combinations of drugs are often required in treating rheumatic diseases. Furthermore, the majority of drugs used to manage rheumatic diseases have side effects which can often be avoided by pre-emptive treatment with other agents eg. prevention of steroid induced osteoporosis with a bisphosphonate.

▶ It is essential that patients be counseled on the potential side effects and appropriate monitoring of these drugs. Drug choices may have to be modified according to patient acceptance and willingness to adhere to monitoring regimens.

The following drugs will be reviewed in this section. This is merely an overview to the use of these drugs, and further reading or consultation with a rheumatologist will be required for optimal use of these agents.

▸▸ NSAIDS
▸▸ Corticosteroids
▸▸ DMARDS
▸▸ Biologics
▸▸ Alternative Agents

Management of specific diseases and use of specific agents is not covered in this chapter, but several references address some of these diseases.

NSAIDS

Uses

In rheumatology, NSAIDS are used primarily for their analgesic and anti-inflammatory properties.

Generally they are used for symptomatic relief, but do not have disease modifying properties for chronic inflammatory conditions. In acute inflammatory conditions (eg. bursitis, acute crystal arthritis) they may be sufficient therapy alone.

There are several classes of these drugs based on their structure. It has been found empirically that if a drug from one class is ineffective, a different NSAID may be tried with better effect.

The primary site of NSAID action is the cyclo-oxygenase enzyme that converts arachidonic acid into prostaglandins, which play an important role in mediating inflammation and pain. Two forms of this enzyme have been described, Cox I and Cox II . Cox I is normally present in high concentrations in platelets, vascular endothelial cells, stomach and kidney collecting tubules, and is responsible for the production of prostaglandins that are essential for maintenance of normal endocrine and renal function, gastric mucosal integrity and hemostasis. In contrast, Cox II is virtually undetectable in most tissues under physiological conditions but its activity is up-regulated by inflammatory stimuli. Cox II is important in synthesis of some inflammatory eicosanoids and prostacyclin, an important mediator of vasodilation. NSAIDs do not suppress leukotriene synthesis by lipoxygenase pathways.

Non-selective NSAIDs inhibit both types of cyclooxygenases (COX-1 and COX-2).

The gastrointestinal adverse events associated with NSAIDs are thought to be due at least in part to inhibition of the Cox I isoform and negative effects on gastric mucosa. It was hypothesised that the selective inhibition of Cox II could reduce the incidence of toxicity, while maintaining the therapeutic efficacy. This led to the development of a new class of NSAID - COX-2 selective inhibitors or the coxibs. These are noncompetitive inhibitors of cyclooxygenase (COX)-2 isoenzyme only, even at supra-therapeutic doses. Due to the selective COX-2 inhibitory activity, coxibs do not inhibit platelet aggregation as seen with aspirin or other non-selective NSAIDs. There is no evidence for superior efficacy of pain relief.

Side effects

Gastrointestinal

The risk of hospitalization due to peptic ulcer complication is about 0.2% per year in non-users of NSAIDs.

Baseline incidence is increased 4-fold in patients currently taking NSAIDs. The risk varies widely with different NSAIDS. The highest risk exists in the first 3 months of therapy.

Identified risk factors for clinical upper gastrointestinal events include prior history of upper GI event (ulcers and complications), age > 70 years, multiple NSAID use (incl. ASA), high-dose NSAIDs, concomitant anticoagulant use, low dose ASA, concomitant corticosteroid use, history of heart disease.

Compared to non-selective NSAIDs, coxibs are associated with lower risk of upper GI events (level I and II evidence- Large trials with these drugs supported some increased safety with respect to the gastrointestinal side effects).

Current guidelines recommend that patients at risk for ulcer disease who require treatment for arthritis receive the combination of a nonselective NSAID with a proton-pump inhibitor or misoprostol. A coxib may be used if cardiovascular risk is acceptable.

Renal/Circulatory

Renal effects reported with all NSAIDs including coxibs include, hypertension, edema, congestive heart failure, worsening renal insufficiency and acute renal failure, hyponatremia, hyperkalemia/type 4 RTA, acute tubulointerstitial nephritis, acute papillary necrosis.

Prostaglandins (PGs) act locally in the kidney to maintain homeostasis by regulating sodium and water reabsorption, particularly in the thick ascending loop of Henle and the collecting duct. NSAIDs, through prostaglandin inhibition increase sodium and water retention by increasing the tubular reabsorption of sodium.

Increases in systolic blood pressure may be associated with treatment with NSAIDs. Most patients with hypertension will not aggravate their blood pressure when an NSAID is initiated, but large increases in systolic (more than diastolic) BP can occur in at-risk patients. Individuals at risk include those with hypertension, or borderline hypertension. Risk may be increased in the elderly and would rarely occur in healthy normotensive patients. Some NSAIDs/Coxibs may do this more than others so BP should be monitored in all chronic NSAID users. No significant alteration in systolic and diastolic blood pressure should be anticipated if patients are switched from a nonselective NSAID to therapeutic doses of COX-2 inhibitors. In a small number of patients, however, the increase in blood pressure with prolonged therapy with nonselective NSAIDs or COX-2 inhibitors may be significant, resulting in development of hypertension.

Patients considered at high risk for adverse renal events, such as those treated with diuretics and ACE inhibitors or AT1-receptor blockers, volume depleted patients, the elderly and patients with CHF or DM, lupus or renal and hepatic insufficiency should be treated cautiously with coxibs as well as non-selective NSAIDs. If treated with these drugs, they should be carefully monitored for edema, hypertension, hyperkalemia and renal failure. NSAIDs may attenuate the effects of antihypertensive medication (particularly those taking ACE inhibitors) through a variety of mechanisms, including renal mechanisms and peripheral vasoactive mechanisms. Doses of antihypertensives may need to be adjusted for patients on concurrent NSAID treatment.

Cardiovascular

Increasing evidence suggests that there is increased risk for serious thrombotic events and myocardial infarction in patients using coxibs for prolonged periods. Therefore, these drugs should be included as a risk factor for cardiovascular events and they should be avoided in patients with other risk factors.

TOPICAL NSAIDS

A preparation of topical Diclofenac has been made available in Canada. This is recommended for management of OA of the knee. It appears that it is comparable to oral diclofenac in efficacy with a significantly lower incidence of GI side effects and laboratory abnormalities. The safety of this agent in patients with hypertension, renal failure and liver disease has not been established.

CORTICOSTERIODS

Uses

These drugs are an important part of the armamentarium of the rheumatologist. There are two main indications for steroids.

1. Suppression of the inflammatory cascade

2. Modification of the immune response

For most systemic inflammatory diseases these play an important role in initial management of life-threatening or severe disease.

High dose therapy: 40mg/d up to 1 mg/kg/d

Recall that Prednisone 5mg = Methylprednisolone (solumedrol) 4mg = Hydrocortisone (solucortef) 20 mg. Initial therapy may be given IV (use conversion to solumedrol) in very ill patients or when oral route cannot be used. High dose therapy is usually continued for a month before proceeding with a taper.

Settings in which this would be considered are systemic vasculitis with organ involvement, such as Wegener's, PAN or temporal arteritis (cutaneous limited vasculitis may not require steroid therapy), SLE flare involving kidney, CNS, mononeuritis multiplex, transverse myelitis, lung or other significant organ involvement, rheumatoid vasculitis, polymyositis/dermatomyositis.

Pulse therapy (such as solumedrol 1g iv OD for 3 days) is a unique way of giving very high doses of corticosteroid over a short period of time, with the intention of rapidly suppressing an acute inflammatory process - it may be considered in any of the above conditions when the disease is producing life-threatening or organ threatening complications. After the pulse therapy, high dose therapy is resumed.

Low or moderate dose therapy may be used for less severe disease or in other conditions.

Most consider low dose corticosteroid to be <15mg prednisone. Moderate dose is 15-40 mg.

Settings in which this dosing would be considered: SLE with less significant organ involvement, vasculitis with less significant organ involvement, polymyalgia rheumatica, as adjunctive therapy in severe rheumatoid arthritis while waiting for other DMARDS to work (low dose only).

Tapering corticosteroids

Once disease control has been established, high prednisone doses should be tapered to below 15 mg/day. In patients receiving doses of prednisone greater than 30 mg/day, the dose can be tapered relatively rapidly at rates of 5 to 10 mg/week. When the dose is below 20 mg/day, the dose should be tapered by 2.5 to 5 mg every 2 to 4 weeks. When patients are taking 10 mg or less, the usual practice is to taper prednisone in 1 to 2.5mg decrements each month.

This requires attention to the disease activity, therefore measures of the disease must be established at the outset, to determine if the disease is flaring as prednisone is tapered. Objective measures (laboratory indices and clinical measures) can be used.

Note that some patients will experience a steroid withdrawal phenomenon, where they experience aching, stiffness and generally feeling unwell during the initial week or two of transition to a lower dose of prednisone.

Perioperative Glucocorticoid Coverage

Supplemental glucocorticoid coverage should be considered for any patient who has received corticosteroids for more than a few weeks in the previous year. Generally , supplemental steroids are administered to all patients who have been taking glucocorticoids who are seriously ill or undergoing major surgery. It is possible to test the integrity of the HPA axis using an ACTH stimulation test. However, this test not done routinely.

Physiologic cortisol secretion in response to major surgery is approximately 75 to 150 mg/day. Return to baseline occurs 24 to 48 hours after surgery. The traditional perioperative protocol gives hydrocortisone, 100 mg with anaesthetic induction and then q8h thereafter for up to 72 hours. An alternate protocol provides patients with the usual dose of oral prednisone on the day of surgery followed by 25 to 50 mg of hydrocortisone immediately preoperatively and every 8 hours thereafter for 48 to 72 hours. For minor or moderate surgical procedures patients can return to their usual prednisone dose on the second postoperative day. For most moderately severe acute illnesses, continuation of the current dose of corticosteroids is adequate.

Adverse effects

Adverse effects of corticosteroids are largely related to dose and duration of therapy.

Some of the adverse effects include:

Glucose intolerance
Edema and hypertension
Osteoporosis (doses >5-7.5 mg/d) (50% of patients will lose bone mass)
Weight gain/obesity
Skin manifestations (easy bruising, striae, impaired wound healing)
Cataract formation (even with 5mg/d)
Avascular necrosis
Infection (doses >.3 mg/kg)
Hirsuitism
Abnormal menstruation
Mood swings/mental disturbances
Muscle weakness (doses >10-20 mg/d)
Peptic ulcer disease (when combined with NSAIDs)

Most adverse effects are not preventable but do require close monitoring. Institution of therapy to prevent glucocorticoid-induced osteoporosis should be considered (please see chapter on osteoporosis).

Intra-articular steroids

The judicious use of this form of steroid therapy can provide excellent relief of inflammatory arthritis in the setting of non-infectious mono- or polyarthritis. This may also allow one to avoid initiating systemic corticosteroids.

Indications

Monoarthritis or disproportionate joint inflammation (after joint infection is ruled out)
Recurrent joint effusion
Tendon sheath inflammation
Bursitis or tendonitis refractory to NSAIDs

However, the operator should be confident about how to enter the joint (see chapter on joint injection techniques).

Complications of steroid injection

Infection (rare, but must ensure aseptic technique, avoidance of infected skin lesion or open wounds around the joint). Artificial joints should generally not be injected.

Hypopigmentation of local skin.

Subcutaneous tissue atrophy.

Tendon rupture may occur if steroid is injected into the surrounding tendons rather than the joint - ensure that fluid can be withdrawn before injecting, and do not continue if resistance is met during the injection-withdraw slightly and re-position the needle.

Steroid crystal-induced synovitis (post-injection flare).

Cartilage damage/tendon weakening- a theoretical risk if injections given more than every 3-4 months.

There is some suppression of cortisol levels for up to 7 days post-injection but this is rarely clinically relevant.

Transient elevation of blood sugar may occur in diabetics.

Other considerations

Patient acceptance of injection
Coagulopathies
Pre-existing joint instability
Lack of response to previous injections
Accessibility of joint
Presence of infection locally or systemically

Preparations

Dexamethasone sodium phosphate (Decadron)	Fast onset, shorter duration of action
Methylprednisolone acetate - Depomedrol	Intermediate onset, duration up to 3-4 months or longer
Triamcinolone acetonide - Aristospan, kenalog	Slower onset, prolonged duration of action

For Depomedrol, typical dose for individual joints:

Finger (MCP,PIP) = 10mg
Wrist = 20 mg

Elbow = 20-40
Shoulder = 40mg
Hip = 80-120mg
Knee = 40-80mg
Ankle = 40 mg

Anaesthetic preparations can be safely mixed with corticosteroid preparations, but the total volume must be kept in mind- overdistending the joint should be avoided.

DMARDS

This refers to drugs that have a disease modifying effect, in that they slow the progress or damage induced by a particular disease. This term has primarily been used in the literature regarding rheumatoid arthritis - these are drugs which have been shown to prevent or slow erosive radiologic change.

In practice, for non-RA diseases, many of these same drugs are used as "steroid sparing" agents to modify the immune response and allow the dose of prednisone to be substantially tapered or discontinued.

The most commonly used DMARDS are:

Plaquenil
Sulfasalazine
Methotrexate
Azathioprine (Imuran)
Myochrysine
Leflunomide (Arava)
Cyclophosphamide (Cytoxan)
Cyclosporin (Neoral)
Mycophenalate Mofetil (Cellcept)
D-penicillamine (rarely used)
Minocycline

Details of these drugs are beyond the scope of this book. Several resources are listed at the end of the chapter.

General concepts of DMARD use:

▶ Ensure that you are clear on the diagnosis and the indications for DMARD choice

▶ Decide on your endpoints for concluding treatment success or failure

▶ Review side effect profile and drug interactions with patient

▶ Ensure pregnancy risks/contraception/fertility have been discussed

▶ Organize appropriate screening bloodwork/urinalysis or other necessary testing for baseline and regular monitoring for drug toxicity

▶ Treatment with these drugs is best done in partnership with a rheumatologist

Drug	Common uses	Side Effects	Monitoring
Plaquenil	Early RA, SLE, rash in DM	Ocular toxicity	Yearly field tests with ophthalmologist +home test
Sulfasalazine	RA, PsA and other seronegative with peripheral joints	GI, rash, bone marrow suppression, hepatic (rare)	Monthly blood work for CBC, Liver enzymes
Methotrexate	RA, PsA, Steroid sparing in SLE, some vasculitis, myositis	Elevated liver enzymes, bone marrow suppression, pneumonitis (rare)Use with Folic acid	Monthly blood work for CBC, AST, ALT, creatinine
Leflunomide	RA, PsA	Elevated liver enzymes, bone marrow suppression, GI toxicity	Monthly blood work for CBC, AST, ALT
Myochrysine	RA (uncommonly used)	Rash, cytopenias, membranous nephritis	Monthly CBC, liver enzymes, creatinine and urinalysis
Cyclophosphamide	Serious manifestations of SLE, vasculitis	Infection, cytopenias, hemorrhagic cystitis, infertility	Regular CBC, urinalysis and cytology q3-6 months
Mycophenalate Mofetil	Role in management of lupus nephritis is evolving	Infection, cytopenias	Regular CBC, liver enzymes
Imuran	SLE, some vasculitis, (RA)	cytopenias, infection, hepatic toxicity (rare)	Monthly bloodwork for CBC, AST, ALT

BIOLOGICS

These newer agents work by inhibiting specific molecular pathways involved in inflammation. The current biologics available inhibit TNFα (infliximab (Remicade ®), etanercept (Enbrel ®), adalimumab (Humira ®)) or IL-1 (anakinra (Kineret ®)). Therefore, their rational use depends on understanding disease pathogenesis, and whether these pathways are relevant in the disease. These drugs are being used primarily for rheumatoid arthritis, but their use has been extended to include psoriatic arthritis and ankylosing spondylitis, in the case of disease refractory to other DMARDS.

There are currently many off-label trials of these drugs in vasculitis and other diseases, and a broader range of therapeutic uses will likely evolve over time.

Other biologics are under study at this time:

Rituximab is an anti-CD20 (B cell) antibody which has an important role in hematologic diseases. It is being studied in RA, because it is partially a B cell driven disease and in SLE, where B cells play a prominent role.

CTLA-Ig is also being investigated in RA- inhibition of the costimulatory molecule CD28, needed for T cell activation.

ALTERNATIVE AGENTS

In general, there is evidence lacking to support the use of any of these preparations in the routine management of rheumatic diseases (OA specifically).

Glucosamine Sulfate

A series of meta-analyses initially suggested that this nutritional supplement was beneficial in OA of the knees. However, there were methodologic problems with these studies. Subsequent, independent studies have not supported its efficacy.

Chondroitin 4-sulphate
S-adenosylmethionine (SAM-E)
Anti-oxidant vitamins (E, C and A)
Fish and Plant Oils
Many others

No demonstrated benefit in OA.

REFERENCES

Therapy of the rheumatic diseases is constantly evolving. The standard references in the introduction provide a good starting point. Up to Date © is updated regularly and will reflect current evidence and trends. Some references from the literature have been provided here as well. The reader is referred to the journals listed in the introduction for the most current reviews and updates.

1. Drug Therapy: New Drugs for Rheumatoid Arthritis. Olsen NJ, Stein CM, NEJM 2004; 350:2167-2179, May 20, 2004

2. Drug Therapy: Therapeutic Strategies for Rheumatoid Arthritis. O'Dell JR, NEJM 2004; 350: 2591-2602, June 17 2004

3. Guidelines for the Management of Rheumatoid Arthritis. 2002 Update American College of Rheumatology Subcommittee on Rheumatoid Arthritis Guidelines, Arthritis and Rheumatism 46(2): 328-346, 2002

4. EULAR Recommendations 2003: an evidence based approach to the management of knee osteoarthritis. Jordan KM, Arden NK, Doherty M, et al., Annals of the Rheumatic Diseases 62(12): 1145-55, Dec 2003

5. Nonsteroidal anti-inflammatory drugs or acetaminophen for osteoarthritis of the hip or knee? A systematic review of evidence and guidelines. Journal of Rheumatology 31(2): 344-54, Feb 2004

6. Gout, Terkeltaub, RA, NEJM 2003; 349: 1647-1655 Oct 23, 2003

Please also see standard references listed in the introduction.

[Section 5]
Selected Rheumatologic Emergencies

[12] Septic Arthritis, Bursitis, Tenosynovitis and Osteomyelitis

Dr. Susan Humphrey-Murto, University of Ottawa

KEY CONCEPTS

These entities are often managed on the General Medical ward, and awareness of diagnosis and management are essential to preserve joint function and life. This chapter includes a more in-depth review of septic arthritis and osteomyelitis, and a less detailed approach to septic bursitis and tenosynovitis. Remember, septic arthritis is one of the few "emergencies" in rheumatology. Always consider it in your differential diagnosis of arthritis.

This section will cover:

1. Septic arthritis; Nongonococcal (NGC) and gonococcal (GC)
2. Osteomyelitis
3. Septic bursitis
4. Flexor tenosynovitis

[12.1] Septic Arthritis
Dr. Susan Humphrey-Murto, University of Ottawa

KEY CONCEPTS

▶ Suspect infection in any inflamed joint.

▶ Failure to diagnose and treat may lead to joint destruction and death.

▶ It is helpful to divide septic arthritis in 2 categories : Nongonococcal (NGC) and gonococcal (GC)

▶ Gonococcal septic arthritis responds very quickly to antibiotics and has an excellent prognosis. NGC septic arthritis may lead to rapid joint damage and a significant increase in morbidity and mortality.

▶ Arthrocentesis is essential for diagnosis.

▶ Treatment of infection requires drainage in addition to antibiotics.

▶ Consult orthopedics for suspected infection in hips, difficult to drain joints, prosthetic joints and previously damaged or arthritic joints. Also consider orthopaedic intervention early on in the immunocompromised individual.

HISTORY

Patient demographics

▶ Any age, but neonates and the elderly are at higher risk.
▶ Diseased joints more easily infected than normal joints. Increased incidence of infection in RA, OA, Charcot joint, crystal induced arthritis.
▶ Risk factors;
  ▸ Systemic diseases like DM, RA, liver disease, alcoholism, chronic renal failure, cancer, malignancy, intravenous drug use (IVDU), immunosuppressive medication.
  ▸ Recent joint surgery, prosthetic joints (incidence of infection 0.1 to 3.5%)
  ▸ Intra-articular steroids (incidence of infection is 0.0002%)
  ▸ An infectious source can be found in 50%.
  ▸ Skin infection, pneumonia, and pyelonephritis are the most commonly identified infectious sources. Consider endocarditis.
▶ In young sexually active persons suspect GC.

Key Questions

1. What is the nature of the joint involvement and distribution?

▶ The typical presentation of septic arthritis is acute pain and swelling in a single joint. It may be polyarticular in 15%.
▶ In the elderly and immunocompromised hosts, septic arthritis may be insidious.
▶ Any joint may be involved but most common in the knee and hip. Axial joints such as the sternoclavicular or sacroiliac joints more common in IVDU or dialysis patients.
▶ In patients with underlying inflammatory arthritis, joint swelling and pain may be out of keeping with prior episodes of arthritis, but immunosuppressive medications may mask symptoms.

2. Have there been any recent infections? Any traumatic injuries or instrumentation (especially near the joints)?

Septic arthritis is often hematogenous in origin, but local introduction of bacteria can also occur.

3. Is the involved joint prosthetic?

▶ Prosthetic joints- early infections have typical signs and symptoms, late infections only joint pain.

4. Sexual history?

- ► Disseminated Gonococcal Infection (DGI) presents as two distinct syndromes:
  1. migratory polyarthritis, tenosynovitis and dermatitis which reflects bacteremia and
  2. localized septic arthritis.

- ► In DGI asymmetric involvement of joints; knee, elbow, wrist, MCP, ankle. Dermatitis consists of a painless maculopapular, pustular, or vesicular rash on an erythematous base.

Medications

- ► Steroids and immunosuppressive agents may mask signs and symptoms of inflammation, prior antibiotics may affect culture results.

Physical Examination

General

- ► Suspect infection if fever, toxic looking, extrarticular site of infection.
- ► Usually febrile, but may be absent in immunocompromised host or the elderly.

MSK

- ► Septic arthritis is PAINFUL and patient will allow very little movement if any of the joint.
- ► Septic joints are effused and usually quite warm. Some are red and hot. If fungal infection, may just have an effusion.

Derm

- ► Examine the skin for pustules (GC), IV access with local infection, or cellulitis. The latter two may be primary sites of infection.

CVS

- ► Look for signs of endocarditis.

GU

- ► Urethritis and cervicitis may be found with GC.

KEY LABORATORY TESTING

CBC - may see increased WBC with left shift

ESR - not specific but suggestive of a significant inflammatory process

Aspirate the affected joint

- ▶ Use an 18 gauge needle as pus may be thick!
- ▶ If you can't aspirate the joint consult rheumatology or orthopedics urgently.
- ▶ For hips aspiration can be done by radiology under fluoroscopic guidance.
- ▶ WBC in synovial fluid often greater than 50,000 WBC/m3.
- ▶ NGC Gram stain + in 70%, GC culture positive in 44%.

Synovial fluid cultures

- ▶ NGC septic arthritis: 75% gram positive cocci, 15% gram negative bacilli. See Table 1 for most commonly found organisms.
- ▶ Mycobacterial and fungal arthritis are much less common than bacterial arthritis, but have been seen more often in the context of HIV infection. An indolent monoarthritis is often the only symptom and synovial membrane histopathology and culture are frequently required to establish the diagnosis.
- ▶ Ten percent of cases never confirmed with blood or synovial fluid cultures.

Blood cultures

- ▶ Blood cultures positive in 50% of NGC arthritis, 13% of GC arthritis

Other cultures

- ▶ In suspected GC also do urethral or cervical cultures (positive in 86%), rectal cultures (39%), throat (7%).

IMAGING

Plain films serve as a baseline and can identify underlying joint disease. Early on will only demonstrate synovial effusion and soft tissue swelling. Consider CT scanning for joints which are difficult to examine such as the hip and sacroiliac joint.

DIFFERENTIAL DIAGNOSIS

- ▶ See section 2:1 on acute monoarthritis
- ▶ There are several reports of co-existing septic arthritis and crystals, so one should beware if this presentation is different than the patient's "usual" symptoms of crystal arthropathy.

TREATMENT

Antibiotics

See table 2 for antibiotic choices.
Start immediately after cultures sent.

Drainage

- ▶ There are no prospective randomized studies that clearly demonstrate surgery is superior to repeated aspirations.
- ▶ Orthopedics should be consulted for hips, previously damaged joints, difficult to aspirate joints such as the sternoclavicular or sacroiliac joints, anytime there is difficulty removing pus by needle aspiration and any joint not responding to treatment.
- ▶ Closed drainage (i.e. needle aspiration) once to several times daily may be adequate for many cases. Knees tend to require daily to twice daily aspirations for 7-10 days.

Hold immunosuppressive drugs, steroids must be continued (use stress doses if appropriate)

Table 1: Septic Arthritis

Organism	Clinical Clues	Who is at risk?
Staphylococcus aureus	Most common organism for all NGC septic arthritis, secondary to bacteremia.	Native and prosthetic joints. Especially common in DM, RA, can be in healthy adults.
Streptococci, pneumococcus	Recent Strep infection such as pneumonia	Often immunocompromised host, can be healthy adults.
Staph epidermidis		Prosthetic joints
E Coli	UTI	IVDU, elderly, immunosuppressed
Pasteurella multocida	Cat bite	
Pseudomonas aeruginosa	Nail in foot	
Gonococcus	Polyarticular arthralgias followed by mono or oligoarticular synovitis, tenosynovitis, pustular eruption	Sexually active, young healthy adults
TB, Fungal	Chronic monoarthritis	HIV, from endemic area, immunosuppressed

Table 2: Suggested antibiotic choice for septic arthritis (it is recommended that you also check your local Infectious Disease service recommendations)

Clues	Suggested antibiotic	Alternatives or expected response
Young sexually active	Ceftriaxone 1g IV or IM (first dose) followed by Ciprofloxacin 500mg po BID x 7d Add Doxycycline 100mg po BID x 7 d to cover possible Chlamydia	Tends to respond very quickly. Once clinically improving x 48hrs, switch to oral Rx with Ciprofloxacin. Even purulent effusions do not result in joint damage.
Any age, do not suspect GC	Cloxacillin or cefazolin 1-2 g IV q8h	
Gram positives on gram stain	Cefazolin 1-2g IV q8h	If from institutional setting consider Vancomycin
Gram negatives on gram stain	3rd generation cephalosporin eg. Cefotaxime 2 g IV q8h	
Pseudomonas suspected	Ceftazidime and Gentamycin	

- General guideline for length of treatment is 14 days IV followed by 14 days po.
- For more virulent pathogens (like Staph Aureus) treat for 3-4 weeks IV.
- Repeated SF analysis should reveal decreasing percentage of neutrophils, WBC count and negative gram stain and cultures.
- Consult occupational therapy for splints, as immobilization in the early stages decreases discomfort.
- Consult physiotherapy for early range of motion of the joint to prevent contractures. Usually should be started 24-48 hours after symptoms subsiding.

[12.2] Osteomyelitis (OM)

Dr. Susan Humphrey-Murto, University of Ottawa

KEY CONCEPTS

- ▶ Consider the diagnosis in any patient with bone pain and fever.
- ▶ OM can be difficult to diagnose. Symptoms and signs may be vague and WBC count may be normal.
- ▶ Usually the ESR is elevated.
- ▶ Initial imaging with Xray followed by bone scan. MRI, if available, is the test of choice.
- ▶ The gold standard for diagnosis is a bone biopsy.
- ▶ If the patient is stable, wait for a positive culture (blood or bone) PRIOR to initiation of antibiotics.

DEFINITION AND HPI

Osteomyelitis (OM) is an infection of the bone. It can arise from hematogenous spread, secondary to a contiguous focus of infection and may be associated with vascular insufficiency.

▶ Although strict criteria are lacking, clinically can be divided in acute (prior to the development of necrotic bone, tend to have more acute presentation with fever and pain), subacute (longer duration of symptoms, pain less severe, minimal fever) and chronic (presence of necrotic bone).

▶ In chronic osteomyelitis characteristic findings include the sequestrum (dead bone), involucrum (reactive bony encasement of the sequestrum), local osteopenia, persistent drainage and sinus tracts. Patients tend to have "recurrent" infection.

▶ Patients may present with fever and localized pain or with general malaise and weight loss. The pain may develop very insidiously and diabetics may have very little pain secondary to neuropathy.

▶ Hematogenous spread of bacteria affects spine (lumbar>thoracic and cervical), pelvis and small bones preferentially. Ask about recent infections and complete a thorough review of systems to search for infections.

▶ Long bone involvement is usually due to open fractures.

▶ OM may lead to local abcess formation such as a paraspinal or epidural abcess with neurologic involvement.

PHYSICAL EXAM

▶ The following may or may not be present; fever, localized tenderness, localized swelling. Often very little to find at bedside. Look for prior trauma, decubitus ulcer, other infections that may have lead to bacteremia. Diabetic foot ulcers that are probed down to bone should be considered to have OM.

KEY LABORATORY TESTING

▶ Increased WBC in acute, but not chronic OM. ESR is usually elevated and is a good marker for following response to treatment. Blood cultures positive in 50%.

▶ For microbiology see Table 3.

IMAGING

▶ Diagnosis- no noninvasive test can definitely establish a diagnosis of OM. A definitive diagnosis requires a bone biopsy. However, suggestive imaging in the setting of a positive blood culture is highly suggestive and is considered by many clinicians to be sufficient for the diagnosis.

▶ Plain films should be taken as a first step. They may suggest the correct diagnosis, exclude other pathology and serve as baseline. Bone destruction and periosteal reaction will only be present after 1-2 weeks. In chronic OM bone sclerosis, periosteal new bone formation and sequestra are seen.

▶ Three phase bone scan should be performed next. There is an initial flow phase, blood pool phase (10 minutes) and delayed static imaging (3 hours). In cellulitis the first 2 phases show increased uptake, whereas in OM intense uptake in all 3 phases. If negative, excludes OM. Useful for detecting multifocal involvement.

▶ Gallium scan- more specific, but less sensitive than the bone scan. Combination in some centers of bone and gallium scan may be helpful. Always best to speak to your local nuclear medicine physicians if in doubt.

▶ White blood cell scan (WBSC) better but not always available. If available, after plain films start with WBCS and if positive go on to bone scan to assess if inflammation coming from the bone. If negative rules out OM.

▶ CT scan can be used to evaluate focal findings. Less sensitive than bone scan and MRI.

▶ MRI is the test of choice if available. Extremely sensitive in the early detection of OM. Sensitivity 82-100% and specificity 75-96%. Also excellent for visualizing soft tissues which may contain abcess, or spinal cord impingement. Because of limited availability, usually necessary to begin with a plain film and bone scan.

▶ Gold standard is an open bone biopsy. Can begin with needle biopsy and, if required, open biopsy.

TREATMENT

▶ If acute OM is not treated adequately there is a risk of developing chronic OM which is less responsive to therapy.

▶ Antibiotics should be started ONLY AFTER appropriate cultures have been sent. A specific microbiologic diagnosis is essential. Organisms isolated from sinus tract drainage may not accurately reflect organisms present in the bone. If blood cultures are negative, do a bone biopsy prior to empiric antibiotics. If the patient appears toxic, you may need to treat prior to bone biopsy, but usually a more indolent presentation and better to establish a definitive microbiologic diagnosis.

▶ Choice of antibiotics will depend on culture results. Empiric choices listed in Table 3.

▶ Usually require 4 to 6 weeks of IV antibiotics, some centers will give 2 weeks of IV antibiotics followed by 4 weeks of po.

▶ Surgery should be consulted especially for patients who are not responding to antibiotics after 48 hrs, have a soft tissue abscess (including epidural abscess), concomitant joint infection or instability of the spine is present.

▶ Consider infectious disease consultation.

Table 3: Osteomyelitis

Mechanism for development of osteomyelitis	Typical organisms	Notes	Who?	Antibiotic pending cultures
Hematogenous	Staph aureus, coag negative Staph, gram negative bacilli (Pseudomonas aeruginosa, Serratia marcescens, E. coli	Usually only one infective agent. Axial skeleton in adults (vertebrae, sternoclavicular, sacroiliac), long bones in children.	Childhood and in patients over 50.	Cloxacillin or cefazolin
Contiguous focus	Staph aureus, coag negative Staph, Streptococcus pyogenes, Enterococcus, gram negative bacilli, anaerobes	polymicrobial		Cloxacillin and Ciprofloxacin
Vascular insufficiency	Staph aureus, Streptococcus sp., Proteus mirabilis, Pseudomonas aeruginosa, anaerobes	polymicrobial		Clavulin if relatively well, if sick meropenum or pip/tazo

[12.3] Septic Bursitis

Dr. Susan Humphrey-Murto, University of Ottawa

KEY CONCEPTS

▶ Most common sites are the olecranon, prepatellar and superficial infrapatellar bursae.

▶ May result from local cutaneous trauma (mild) leading to direct inoculation, or by spread of cellulitis. Only 8% of patients are bacteremic.

▶ An important key on history is where the pain and redness started. With bursitis, patients will point to the center of the bursa and often describe redness starting there and spreading out. In contrast with arthritis where the patient points to the joint in a diffuse fashion.

▶ Often may have extensive cellulitis but does not involve the joint. Therefore despite impressive local pain, swelling and erythema, joint movement relatively painless. Maximal point of tenderness is over the center of the bursa.

▶ Try aspirating fluid for diagnosis and treatment. Just put the 18 gauge needle in the most fluctuant portion (after proper sterile technique and freezing, of course). Try to avoid puncturing in the most dependent or stressed area of the bursa, as chronic drainage could result. Approach the fluctuant portion indirectly from a lower stress aspect of the bursa.

▶ Culture is positive in 15-50% of patients.

▶ Usually gram positives, over 80% Staph aureus, remainder is Steptococcus.

▶ Gram negatives are rare. Fungal and TB may lead to indolent chronic infections.

▶ Rx consists of antibiotics. Repeated aspiration should be attempted but in my experience are often "dry". Usually responds very well to antibiotics and only rarely would require surgical drainage. Consult surgery if suspect a foreign body or worsening clinical picture despite antibiotics.

[12.4] Acute and Chronic Flexor Tenosynovitis

Dr. Susan Humphrey-Murto, University of Ottawa

KEY CONCEPTS

► Infection of the closed synovial sheaths of the flexor tendons. May be the result of penetrating trauma or bacteremia.

► Most common organism is Staph aureus. Disseminated gonorrhea may involve multiple tendons simultaneously. Chronic tenosynovitis results from infection with Mycobacterium tuberculosis, Mycobaterium marinum and fungal elements such as histoplasmosis, coccidiomycosis etc.

► Finger held in semiflexion. Volar erythema, swelling and extreme pain on passive extension are present. Passive flexion is relatively painless.

► Treatment involves antibiotics and drainage by plastic surgery.

REFERENCES

1. Orthopedic management of Septic Arthritis, Donatto KC, Rheumatic Disease Clinics of North America, May 1998, 24:2, 275-286.

2. Soft Tissue Disease, Valeriano-Marcet J, Carter JD, Vasey FB, Rheumatic disease clinics of North America, Feb 2003, 29:1, 77-87.

3. Imaging of osteomyelitis and musculoskeletal soft tissue infections: current concepts, Santiago Restrepo C, Giménez CR, McCarthry K, Rheumatic disease clinics of North America, Feb 2003, 29:1, 89-105.

[13] Approach to Giant Cell Arteritis

Dr. David Robinson, University of Manitoba

KEY CONCEPTS

▶ Most common systemic vasculitis in North America

▶ Idiopathic large vessel vasculitis affecting second to fifth branches of aorta

▶ Unlike atherosclerosis, plaque rupture and thrombosis are uncommon

▶ Affects individuals 50 years of age and over

▶ High overlap with polymyalgia rheumatica

▶ Clinical manifestations arise from ischemia in the affected tissues in combination with constitutional symptoms arising from circulating cytokines

▶ There are a number of distinct clinical patterns with which patients can present

▶ Urgent diagnosis and treatment required to prevent abrupt onset of irreversible blindness in small number of cases

HISTORY

Patient Demographics

- ► Occurs almost exclusively in individuals older than 50 years
- ► Women commoner than men
- ► Prevalence highest in those of Northern European descent

Key Questions

For GCA, it is most useful to organize questions to identify one of the four major patterns of presentation.

GCA can present with a number of distinct clinical patterns. There are four major patterns but combinations of findings can occur. Diagnosis often requires careful history and physical examination, and is often difficult.

1. Are there cranial artery symptoms?

A. Headache - New onset of headache or new pattern of headache in the elderly should prompt consideration of GCA. Patients may have scalp tenderness noted when lying down with pressure on their scalp, combing their hair or wearing hats.

B. Jaw claudication - Patients may have discomfort in their temporalis or masseter muscles, or tongue discomfort while talking or chewing. This is usually relieved with rest, similar to claudication in the legs in peripheral vascular disease.

C. Visual changes - Abrupt visual loss may occur due to involvement of the posterior ciliary or ophthalmic arteries supplying the optic nerve. The visual loss is often irreversible and occasionally bilateral but can usually be prevented by adequate steroid therapy.

D. Stroke - Intracranial vessels are usually spared due to lack of an internal elastic lamina. Case reports of stroke due to occlusion of carotid arteries do exist. Exact incidence of stroke in GCA is impossible to determine due to lack of tissue for pathology and high incidence of atheroembolic strokes in this age group.

2. Is there involvement of the aorta or primary branches?

Severe stenosis in the subclavian, carotid, and axillary arteries occurs in 10-15% of patients with GCA. Symptoms at presentation include limb claudication, parasthesias, ischemic changes and Raynaud's phenomenon. Cranial symptoms are typically absent and temporal artery biopsies are usually negative. Constitutional symptoms may be absent.

3. Are there symptoms of polymyalgia rheumatica?

Extremely common in individuals over 50 years of age, PMR is considered by many to be a milder or partial form of GCA. PMR follows or precedes GCA in 40 - 60% of cases and all patients with PMR should be watched for development of GCA. Clinically, patients will present with aching and pain in the neck, pectoral and pelvic girdles. Symptoms are often worse at night and patients describe difficulty turning over in bed with prolonged morning stiffness. Constitutional symptoms of fatigue and malaise are often present. There is no specific diagnostic test. Acute phase reactants are usually elevated. A "Hallelulah" type response (ie: near complete relief) to corticosteroids (20 -30 mg) occurs within hours and helps confirm diagnosis.

4. Is this a FUO (fever of unknown origin)?

GCA may account for a significant proportion of FUO in patients over 65 years of age. In these cases, arteritis occurs without vessel lumen narrowing and tissue ischemia. Fever, malaise, weight loss and night sweats can occur by themselves or in conjunction with either of the presentations described above.

PHYSICAL EXAMINATION

Each of the clinical presentations above has different physical manifestations which should be sought on examination.

1. Are there cranial artery findings?

Check for scalp tenderness, masseter and temporalis tenderness, temporal artery thickening, tenderness or pulselessness. Fundoscopy may be normal or may show pallor or edema of the optic disc, cotton wool patches or small hemorrhages.

2. Is there large vessel involvement?

Check pulses and blood pressures in both arms (legs are less frequently affected). Look for peripheral signs of tissue ischemia. Listen for bruits over large vessels and palpate for an aortic aneurysm.

3. Are there any joint findings?

The exact source of myalgias in PMR is unclear. The presence of actual joint swelling however, is a negative predictor for obtaining a positive temporal artery biopsy and suggests elderly onset rheumatoid arthritis.

4. Are there alternative causes of symptoms?

Physical exam (and history) should always try to elicit alternate causes for the patient's symptoms. In this age group, malignancy and indolent infections can present with chronic constitutional symptoms. PMR is a diagnosis of exclusion.

LABORATORY INVESTIGATIONS

Is there an acute phase response?

Highly elevated erythrocyte sedimentation rates (ESR) are usually found in GCA. C-reactive protein is also elevated and is more specific for the acute phase response than ESR.

Anemia of chronic disease and thrombocytosis are also common.

GCA can occur infrequently with normal acute phase reactants.

Do I need a temporal artery biopsy?

Definite diagnosis of GCA requires pathologic examination of arterial tissue. Temporal artery biopsy is a minimally invasive procedure with few adverse effects. The presence of jaw claudication, diplopia, and an enlarged temporal artery are predictive of positive biopsy result. Conversely, patients with aortitis and no cranial symptoms are unlikely to have a positive biopsy. Because of the presence of skip lesions, a 2-3 cm length of temporal artery should be obtained. If negative, the contralateral artery should be biopsied. Biopsies may be positive after several days of steroid therapy but should not be delayed beyond a week after starting steroids. While it is tempting in certain cases to forgo biopsy, it can be invaluable further on in treatment if the patient develops atypical symptoms or has a poor response to treatment. A biopsy should be performed whenever possible.

Pathology on biopsy: Panarteritis with giant cell granuloma formation. Also look for disruption of internal elastic lamina and intimal thickening. Involvment may be patchy and skip lesions are seen.

IMAGING

Currently, none is used routinely.

Conventional X-ray angiography may show typical stenotic lesions of the subclavian, axillary, proximal brachial or carotid arteries. Aortitis leads to dilatation and aneurysm formation. MRI and CT angiography may be helpful by demonstrating vessel wall thickening. MRI can show edema of the vessel walls characteristic of inflammation.

INITIAL THERAPY

Corticosteroids

Corticosteroids are the mainstay of therapy and should be instituted promptly to avoid vision loss. Usual therapy is with prednisone at 1mg/kg of body weight until symptoms improve (usually 2-4 weeks) and then tapered by 10 mg per week. Once at 20 mg, tapering should be slower (2.5 mg per week), and slower still once 10mg is reached (1 mg q 2-4 weeks) Tapering regimens vary considerably. Return of symptoms or elevation of acute phase reactants should prompt return to previous dose of steroid which controlled symptoms.

Elevation of acute phase reactants alone may not necessarily indicate need for increased steroid if the patient is clinically well. Avoid knee-jerk reaction of increasing steroid based on lab test alone.

Treatment may be prolonged and last several years.

Steroid-Sparing Agents

Conflicting results have been obtained in trials using methotrexate as a steroid-sparing agent in GCA. Inconsistent results have also been found with several other immunosuppressives. Limited data suggests some effect from anti-TNF therapy. Most clinicians will use steroid-sparing agents in patients requiring unacceptably high steroid doses for symptom control. For methotrexate, it appears a minimum of 15 mg/week is required for effect.

Prevention of Complications

Patients should receive prophylaxis for osteoporosis in the form of calcium, vitamin D and anti-resorptive agents. Monitor for cognitive effects of steroids, hypertension and diabetes mellitus.

PITFALLS IN GCA TREATMENT

Problems often arise after patients have started therapy and either fail to respond or flare on fairly large doses of steroid. Most of these questions arise in cases where a positive temporal artery biopsy was not obtained.

Is it all atherosclerosis?

Ubiquitous in this age group, atherosclerotic lesions can mimic many of the symptoms of GCA. ESR may be falsely elevated or increased for other reasons.

Is the ESR reliable?

ESR may not reflect the acute phase response for a number of reasons. Normal ranges on lab sheets may not reflect age-specific upper limit of normal (roughly ½ the patient's age). C-reactive protein may be more specific for inflammation than ESR.

Was the headache vasculitic?

Unfortunately, headaches stemming from a number of non-inflammatory causes (eg: migraine) may improve with corticosteroids and a prompt response to prednisone is not always diagnostic.

REFERENCES

1. Weyand and Goronzy, Ann Intern Med 2003;139:505-515
2. Weyand and Goronzy, N Engl J Med 2003;349:160-169

[14] Pulmonary/Renal Syndrome
Dr. Eric Rich, Université de Montréal

KEY CONCEPTS

▶ Rapidly progressing glomerulonephritis and pulmonary infiltrates/hemorrhage define the Pulmonary-Renal syndromes which are often the manifestation of small-vessel vasculitis

▶ The principal causative diseases are: ANCA-associated vasculitis (Wegener' disease, microscopic polyangiitis (MPA), Churg-Strauss syndrome (CSS), Goodpasture's syndrome, connective tissue diseases (CTD) like SLE

▶ These patients need to be quickly recognized, thoroughly investigated and aggressively treated as they may rapidly become critically ill

▶ Urinalysis, ANCA and antibodies to the glomerular basement membrane (anti-GBM), bronchoscopy, organ biopsy (often kidney) are the core diagnostic tests

▶ Therapy with I.V solumedrol, cyclophosphamide +/- plasmapheresis should not be delayed. Sometimes treatment must be initiated before confirmatory test results are available

▶ It is particularly important to establish a very efficient communication between the many specialties involved in the care of these patients (nephrologists, respirologists, rheumatologists, ICU physicians, radiologists)

HISTORY

The combination of acute renal insufficiency and pulmonary infiltrates/hemorrhage can be seen in more common conditions such as severe pneumonia with acute tubular necrosis, ARDS from sepsis, heart failure with pre-renal impairment, any severe glomerular disease with marked fluid overload and pulmonary edema.

If the clinical picture cannot be attributed to any of these more frequent etiologies, the possibility of small-vessel vasculitis or CTD should be entertained.

Lung capillaritis can lead to alveolar hemorrhage manifested by cough, severe dyspnea and hemoptysis.

Pearl: 1/3 of patients with diffuse alveolar hemorrhage will not have hemoptysis; dyspnea, diffuse pulmonary infiltrates and a dropping hemoglobin will then be your clues.

Rapidly progressive glomerulonephritis may manifest with symptoms of uremia.

Pulmonary-renal syndrome can develop as a flare of an established disease or, more often, as the presenting feature of the following diseases:

ANCA-associated vasculitis

▶ Intense arthralgias and fatigue, low grade fever are common to Wegener's, MPA and CSS
▶ Unusually persistent sinusitis with nasal discharge, recurrent otitis and red eyes are suggestive of Wegener; stridor due to subglottic inflammation should be sought as it can contribute to dyspnea and complicate ventilatory support in critically ill patients. Pre-existent asthma is frequent in CSS
▶ Peripheral nerve involvement is seen in up to 25% of ANCA-associated vasculitis
▶ Check for potential drug-induced vasculitis: propylthiuracil (PTU), minocycline, hydralazine

Goodpasture syndrome

▶ Goodpasture syndrome is less frequent than the ANCA-associated vasculitis.

Pearl: Pulmonary hemorrhage happens almost exclusively in current smokers. Goodpasture's is usually associated with milder preceding systemic symptoms

Connective tissue diseases

▶ Look for SLE symptoms (polyarthralgias, photosensitive rashes, serositis,...), scleroderma

Other rare causes

▶ Other vasculitis (cryoglobulinemia, Henoch-Shonlein), bacterial endocarditis, catastrophic antiphospholipid syndrome, thrombotic thrombocytopenic purpura, hemolytic uremic syndrome

PHYSICAL EXAMINATION

Vitals: always be worried about fever, as sepsis is a frequent mimicker or a superimposed complication; check O2 sat% as rapid transfer to the ICU may be needed for ventilatory monitoring and support.

Eyes: conjunctivitis, episcleritis, scleritis are seen in ANCA-associated vasculitis, SLE.

Skin/mucous membranes: subungual splinters and digital tip ischemic lesions are seen in ANCA-associated vasculitis, SLE, infective endocarditis; malar rash, shallow erythematous ulcers on hard palate in SLE.

Lungs: listen for stridor (Wegener's), diffuse crackles, usually no signs of pleural effusion.

Neurologic: drop foot or wrist in ANCA-associated vasculitis.

LABORATORY INVESTIGATION

▶ **CBC:** an unexplained low and falling hemoglobin may indicate lung hemorrhage

▶ **Creatinine:** follow very carefully, even q 12 hrs initially. Once the creatinine rises in WG, renal failure can develop rapidly

▶ **Urine Analysis:** essential and too often forgotten! Check daily for RBC, RBC casts, protein

▶ **PTT/INR:** look for coagulation perturbation that may aggravate the condition

▶ **Blood/urine/sputum cultures:** as often as needed because infection is a frequent comorbidity in these patients

▶ **Anti-Neutrophil Cytoplasmic Antibodies (ANCA):** very useful!

Pearl: You should obtain ANCA by immunofluorescence (c-ANCA and p-ANCA) and by ELISA (anti-PR3 and anti-MPO); the combination of both increases the sensitivity but mostly the specificity of this test

▸▸ 90% of Wegener's patients are ANCA positive; c-ANCA/anti-PR3 are found in 85% of them and p-ANCA/anti-MPO in the rest

▸▸ 75% of patients with MPA are ANCA positive, almost exclusively p-ANCA/anti-MPO

▸▸ ANCA is less prevalent in CSS (around 60%) and usually p-ANCA/anti-MPO.

▸▸ Initially, ANCA can be negative in Wegener's limited to sinuses but become positive when renal and/or lung involvement appears

▸▸ Be cautious in interpreting p-ANCA with negative anti-MPO as many unrelated conditions can cause this positive test (inflammatory bowel disease, CTD, autoimmune hepatitis...)

▶ **Anti-GBM antibodies:** very useful to diagnose Goodpasture's syndrome; in that condition 50% of patients have only kidney involvement and the other 50% both lung and renal disease

An ELISA for anti-GBM is much more sensitive than immunofluorescence; if the test is not readily available, a kidney biopsy is the right way to make the diagnosis

In 20-40% of anti-GBM positive patients, coexistent ANCA will be identified, more often p-ANCA/anti-MPO; these 'double positive' patients evolve more like ANCA-associated vasculitis

▶ **Anti-nuclear antibodies (ANA):** virtually all SLE patients will be ANA positive; on the contrary, many unrelated conditions can have positive ANA (see chapter on laboratory tests)

IMAGING/PROCEDURES

▶ **Chest X-Ray:** patchy or diffuse alveolar opacities

▶ **Chest CT-Scan:** alveolar ground-glass appearance

▶ **Pulmonary function tests:** classically elevated DLCO due to hemoglobin in the alveolar compartment. Patients often too sick to do PFTs

▶ **Bronchoscopy:** necessary to exclude infection in most cases. Bloody secretions often seen in many lobes. Sequential BAL aspirates will show a progressive hemorrhagic return, suggestive of alveolar hemorrhage. Hemosiderin-laden macrophages will be identified when bleeding has been more chronic and is helpful when overt hemorrhage is not seen despite alveolar infiltrates on x-rays

BIOPSY

The high morbidity of the disease, the toxicity of therapies and the need for long-term treatment make a firm diagnosis essential in pulmonary-renal syndromes. The gold standard is tissue biopsy of an affected organ. In severely ill patients, therapy may have to be initiated before a pathologic diagnosis is available.

Most often, kidney is the preferred site to biopsy as it is less risky than lung biopsy in patients with a limited respiratory reserve and is feasible even in patients on mechanical ventilation; specimens from transbronchial lung biopsy are usually unsatisfactory and non-conclusive.
In Wegener's, sinus biopsy is easily accessible but diagnostic in only 25% of patients. Finally, skin biopsy of 'fresh' purpuric lesions will often show leucocytoclasic vasculitis but will not permit differentiation between the various forms of vascultis.

Kidney biopsy of ANCA-associated vasculitis will show a characteristic pauci-immune necrotizing glomerulonephritis (i.e scant or no immunoglobulins and complement on tissue immunofluorescence). In Goodpasture's, linear deposition of immunoglobulins along the basement membrane with crescentic glomerulonephritis is the standard finding.

THERAPY

▶ Immunosuppresion with high-dose corticosteroids, cyclophosphamide +/- plasmapheresis is the standard treatment of ANCA-associated vasculitis, Goodpasture's and SLE presenting with a pulmonary-renal syndrome; this aggressive regimen is warranted even in dialysis-dependent patients as return of renal function is possible

► Solumedrol 500-1000 mg IV od x 3-5 days followed by 1-2 mg/kg daily (IV or po). Alveolar hemorrhage usually stops after 3-7 days

► Cyclophosphamide should be added for better control, faster tapering of steroids and avoiding relapses. Many administration protocols are possible:

   ➤ 2 mg/kg IV or po od or 1 gm/m2 IV repeated after 2-4 weeks or replaced by 2 mg/kg po od

   ➤ Pulse or daily administration should be adjusted for renal function: if < 15% normal creatinine clearance, 1/2 dose; 15-40%, 2/3 dose; 40-70%, 3/4 dose

   ➤ Carefully check for drug-induced leukopenia (often after the 7th day of treatment), and start lowering/suspending cyclophosphamide when the total WBC count is on a clear downward trend and approaches 4000/mm3 (WBC should be maintained >3500/m3 or 1500/mm3 neutrophils)

► Septra DS 3/week (or its equivalent) should be added in all cases to prevent P. carinii infection. Daily sputum cultures in the ICU patient makes sense and start early empiric antibiotherapy in suspected infection

► Daily plasmapheresis (plasma exchange) should be quickly started in suspected Goodpasture's in order to remove circulating pathogenic anti-GBM antibodies. Levels of anti-GBM are followed until they normalize which usually requires about 14 plasmaphereses. The benefits of plasmapheresis in ANCA-associated vasculitis are less established but this procedure is often used in life-threatening disease, severe kidney disease with dialysis requirement and in the first days of pulmonary hemorrhage when Goodpasture has not yet been ruled out

REFERENCES

1. Rodriguez W et al., Pulmonary-renal syndromes in the intensive care. Critical Care Clinics, vol18 (4),Oct 2002

2. Merkel P et al., Evaluation and treatment of vasculitis in the critically ill patient. Critical Care Clinics, 18 (2) April 2002

[15] Approach to Scleroderma Renal Crisis

Dr. Janet Pope, University of Western Ontario

KEY CONCEPTS

1. SRC consists of some or all of elevated creatinine, evidence of microangiopathic hemolytic anemia, hypertension in the setting of scleroderma (often diffuse disease).

2. SRC is associated with high renins and is like malignant hypertension.

3. SRC is a medical emergency and the more quickly the BP is under control the less likely there will be chronic renal failure and need for dialysis

4. ACE inhibitors are the first line therapy and have decreased the mortality rate of SRC but the mortality of these patients is still high

5. Steroids increase significantly the risk of SRC and should be used only with caution in those with high risks of developing SRC, such as those with rapidly progressing skin involvement

6. SRC is often an acute on chronic condition, so BP should be watched carefully and monitored like pre-eclampsia where a small increase in BP should be considered a warning.

HISTORY

Patient Demographics

► Patients with diffuse and progressing scleroderma are at high risk

► Often they are RNA polymerase positive (but this is not a routine part of the ENA)

► Not all of the features need to be present:

  ▸ HTN

  ▸ Rising creatinine

  ▸ Anemia with intravascular hemolysis: order a peripheral smear and look for schistocytes and other

  ▸ features of RBC breakdown

Key Questions

Note that SRC is asymptomatic initially.

1. History of scleroderma

► Often in first few years of those with diffuse scleroderma

► Often with active disease (worsening skin tightening)

2. Triggers

Ask about steroid use (esp in high dose) as it is an important risk factor. Often SRC exacerbated by other renal insults, such as dehydration (eg. with diuretic use).

PHYSICAL EXAMINATION

General appearance

► Often the patient has diffuse skin change and looks sick.

Vitals

► Usually elevated BP (doesn't have to be).

Skin and nails

► Often obvious scleroderma with diffuse disease.

► Superficial dilated capillaries - telangiectasias or periungual changes.

► Tendon friction rubs.

CVS

► Pericardial effusions are common in SRC (echocardiographically) but often not clinically evident

Respiratory
  ▶ May detect interstitial lung disease (crackles at bases) associated with scleroderma

KEY LABORATORY INVESTIGATION

No tests are confirmatory.

Creatinine: elevated

Urinalysis: usually normal or reveals only mild proteinuria with few cells or casts

Electrolytes: especially K+

CBC, peripheral smear: look for microangiopathic hemolytic anemia, consumptive thrombocytopenia

Plasma renin levels: may be elevated twice the ULN or greater

Renal biopsy: not typically indicated since this does not definitively establish the diagnosis of scleroderma renal disease (will see thrombotic microangiopathy which may also be seen in other non-scleroderma causes of this presentation)

IMAGING

None indicated.

DIFFERENTIAL DIAGNOSIS

▶ Other causes of HTN and renal insuffiency such as NSAIDs superimposed on dehydration

▶ Anemia due to blood loss -common in scleorderma
  ▶▶ erosive esophagitis with bleeding
  ▶▶ bleeding from telangiectasia in a "watermelon stomach"s
  ▶▶ anemia of chronic disease
  ▶▶ intravascular hemolyisis is not common except in SRC (fragmented cells, schistocytes, tear drop cells, etc)

▶ Malignant nephrosclerosis (due to accelerated hypertension), hemolytic-uremic syndrome, thrombotic thrombocytopenic purpura (may have fever and neurologic phenomena), antiphospholipid antibody syndrome (may have multiple organ involvement with ischemia)

INITIAL THERAPY

► ABCs (such as rehydration)

► Rapid control of BP

► Primary drug therapy with with ACE inhibitors (Captopril, Enalapril best studied), but add any antihypertensive to achieve control

  ▶▶ Note that ARB do not appear to have same benefit as ACEI

► Dialysis for K, elevated Creatinine, fluid overload

  ▶▶ If patient goes on dialysis, maintain the ACEI as the kidneys may recover even after several months

► Anemia may need Rx

SRC has a very poor prognosis and often these patients die of their overall scleroderma disease burden in the future.

REFERENCES

1. Seibold JR. Connective tissue diseases characterized by fibrosis. In: Kelley W, Harris E, Ruddy S, Sludge C, eds. Textbook of Rheumatology. 5th ed. Philadelphia: W.B. Saunders Company; 1997. p. 1133-68.

2. Steen VD. Scleroderma renal crisis. Rheum Dis Clin North Am. 2003 May;29(2):315-33. Review.

3. Steen VD, Medsger TA Jr. Long-term outcomes of scleroderma renal crisis. Ann Intern Med. 2000 Oct 17;133(8):600-3.

4. Steen VD, Medsger TA Jr. Case-control study of corticosteroids and other drugs that either precipitate or protect from the development of scleroderma renal crisis. Arthritis Rheum. 1998 Sep;41(9):1613-9.

5. Helfrich DJ, Banner B, Steen VD, Medsger TA Jr. Normotensive renal failure in systemic sclerosis. Arthritis Rheum. 1989 Sep;32(9):1128-34

[Section 6]
Approach to Physical Examination in the Rheumatic Diseases

[16] Approach to the Screening MSK Exam

Dr. Lori Albert, University of Toronto

KEY CONCEPTS

▶ Musculoskeletal problems are common in inpatient and outpatient settings

▶ Attention to other medical problems may lessen time available for a complete rheumatologic assessment

▶ Musculoskeletal disorders may affect patient morbidity and mortality and impair rehabilitation efforts

▶ A screening MSK history and examination will allow the physician to rapidly assess the patient for musculoskeletal problems in the context of their other medical issues

▶ Easy to incorporate in physical exam skill set and use in all patients

GALS SCREENING EXAMINATION

(adapted from Doherty M, Dacre J, Dieppe P, Snaith M, The "GALS" loco-motor screen. Annals of the Rheumatic Disease 1992:51:1165-69)

GALS = Gait, Arms, Legs, Spine

3 Screening Questions:

1. Have you any pain or stiffness in your muscles, joints or back?
2. Can you dress yourself completely without any difficulty?
3. Can you walk up and down stairs without any difficulty?

Screening Examination

- ▶ Patient in underwear

- ▶ Three positions for exam
  - ▶▶ Walking
  - ▶▶ Standing
    - ▷ Back/Side/Front
  - ▶▶ Supine

- ▶ Order not important
  - ▶▶ Incorporate within your usual screening exam

Position/Activity	Observation
Inspection of gait	
Gait	Symmetry, smoothness of movement
	Normal stride length
	Normal heel strike, stance, toe off and swing through
	Ability to turn quickly
Inspection from behind	
Spine	Straight spine (no scoliosis),
	Symmetrical paraspinal muscles
	Normal shoulder and gluteal muscle bulk/symmetry
	Level iliac crests
Legs	No popliteal swelling
	No hindfoot swelling/deformity

Inspection from the side

Spine	Normal cervical and lumbar lordosis
	Normal (mild) thoracic kyphosis
"Touch toes"	Normal lumbar spine (and hip)
	forward flexion

Inspection from the front

Spine

"Head on shoulders"	Normal cervical lateral flexion

Arms

"Arms behind head"	Normal glenohumeral, sternoclavicular and
	acromioclavicular joint movement
"Arms straight"	Full elbow extension
"Hands in front"	No wrist/finger swelling or deformity
	Ability to fully extend fingers
"Squeeze across 2nd-5th MCPs"	Identify pain of synovitis (test gently)
"Turn hands over"	Normal supination/pronation
	(proximal and distal radioulnar joints)
	Normal palms (no swelling, muscle
	wasting, erythema)
"Make a fist"	Normal power grip
"Fingers on thumb"	Normal fine precision pinch/dexterity

Legs

	Normal quadriceps bulk/symmetry
	No knee swelling or deformity
	(varus/valgus)
	No forefoot/midfoot deformity
	Normal arches

Lying down

Legs

Flex each hip and knee	Confirm full flexion and no knee crepitus
Rotate each hip in flexion	Confirm no pain, no restriction
Palpate for effusion	Confirm no knee effusion
Squeeze across MTPS	Identify pain of synovitis
Inspect soles	Identify callosities reflecting
	abnormal weight bearing

Record the screening exam in the following way - this example shows a normal screening examination.

GAIT	✔	APPEARENCE	MOVEMENT
ARMS		✔	✔
LEGS		✔	✔
SPINE		✔	✔

This example shows a "positive" screening examination.

GAIT	✔	APPEARENCE	MOVEMENT
ARMS		✔	✔
LEGS		✔	X*
SPINE		X**	✔

* 10 degree flexion contracture right knee
** mild dextroscoliosis thoracic spine

REFERENCES

1. Doherty M, Dacre J, Dieppe P, Snaith M, The "GALS" locomotor screen. Annals of the Rheumatic Disease 1992:51:1165-69

[17] Approach to the Detailed Joint Examination

Dr. Evelyn Sutton, Dalhousie University

The purpose of this chapter is to provide the reader with a framework for the detailed joint examination if the screening examination suggests specific joint abnormalities. The monitoring of patients with chronic inflammatory arthritis deserves special mention, and the concept of the joint count will be discussed briefly.

KEY CONCEPTS

▶ You do need to remember basic functional anatomy

▶ Approach each joint in an organized fashion, and hypothesis test as you go

▶ Your goal on the examination is to be able to determine whether a joint is normal or abnormal

▶ If abnormal, is it *INFLAMMATORY* or *DEGENERATIVE* joint disease

▶ Joint swelling should be identified as arising from increased intra-articular fluid, hypertrophied synovium(both inflammatory) or from bony enlargement (degenerative).

▶ If you determine that the patient has joint disease, the pattern of joint involvement, the nature of swelling (bony or fluid) and the duration of symptoms will aid in formulating a specific diagnosis.

BASIC PRINCIPLES

If a joint is swollen because of increased fluid, it is:

▶ most likely sore, and the body will consciously or unconsciously try to protect it. The normal movement (range of motion) will be decreased in at least two planes, usually flexion and extension.

▶ warm to the touch

▶ protected, both consciously and unconsciously. A sore, weight-bearing joint will result in an antalgic (pain relieving) gait. A sore upper limb joint will be held close to the body to protect it.

▶ possibly red: erythema is an important sign and indicates inflammation. Characteristically gouty joints are brighter and hotter than rheumatoid joints and even septic joints. If there is desquamation about the joint, gout is nearly always the cause.

Examine all joints using the same approach: **inspection, palpation, range of motion, special tests**.

Inspection: Always compare like joints simultaneously. Make sure you get more than one view; for the hands and wrists, inspect the radial, ulnar, palmer and dorsal planes. Elbows, shoulders hips and knees, ankles- make sure to look anteriorly, posteriorly and laterally. In the feet, don't forget the "worm's eye view" i.e., the sole of the foot, in addition to the top of the foot. Look for alignment, bony or soft tissue swelling, erythema, nodules, skin changes and peri-articular muscle atrophy about all joints.

Palpation: Palpate each joint to identify tenderness, effusions, bony enlargement and crepitus. Assess heat in the wrists, elbows, knees and ankles. Do not waste your time trying to assess heat in the shoulder or hip joints; they are covered by muscle that by nature, is metabolically active, and hence, should be warm. Knees, elbows and ankles however are close to the surface and should be cooler than muscle. Fingers and toes are usually at ambient temperature and temperature evaluation is unreliable.

Identify the important bony and soft tissue landmarks for each major joint. The bony landmarks are particularly important in the evaluation of the swollen joint as they form the reference points needed for proper joint aspiration and/or injection. Next feel for a joint effusion. Palpate the tendon insertions for tenderness, and where present, evaluate the bursae for swelling.

Range of Motion: Active range of motion should be done first. Active ROM that is unrestricted and without protected movements need not be followed up with passive movement of the joints. When active range is restricted, passive range must be assessed. Examination of the hip is unique: one usually skips active range and proceeds directly to passive range of motion.

Special tests:

To test for tendon inflammation/damage: Regardless of name, these tests all utilize the same principle of stretch and stress. If you can vaguely remember where a tendon attaches, you can assess it by putting it under a stretch or a stress. The stretch can be passive or active: if a tendon is inflamed, stretching it will cause pain. Since other structures are also stretched (e.g. skin, superficial nerves) one can test the same tendon by putting it under a stess: ie. resisting muscle-powered movement of the tendon.

To test for ligamentous integrity: These tests are based solely on applying a stretching force across the ligament and evaluating joint movement and patient report of pain. A minimum number of named tests is included in this chapter. They are so well known that the internal medicine resident should ensure he/she is familiar with them.

Joint Count or articular index: This is a summation of the number of "active" joints (inflamed joints) to assist the clinician in monitoring the effectiveness of therapy. A number of different articular indexes for disease activity exist (see references). In clinical practice, the total number of clinically active joints is usually determined by adding the number of swollen joints to the number of joints that are painful or tender on passive movement. When seeing a patient with a chronic inflammatory arthropathy such as rheumatoid arthritis, the active joint count is one of the measures used to determine whether current therapy should be continued or altered. You should be able to evaluate a patient for clinically active joints and summarize with an active joint count.

In addition to documenting a joint count, you should try to record your joint exam using a homunculus:

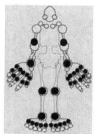 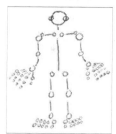

You can easily learn to draw your own homunculus with practice

This gives a complete but easy to read representation of the involved joints, and a diagnostic pattern may become evident. It is also easy to follow clinical improvement if each evaluation is noted in this way.

You should define a legend for your diagram.

Eg: X = tender joint
      ● = effused joint

Note specific deformities

For the example above, this patient has 38 swollen joints, in a pattern suggestive of RA - small and large joints, symmetrically distributed in both lower and upper extremities.

SPECIFIC JOINT EXAMINATION

It is not possible to itemize all the aspects of the MSK exam in this text, but a quick summary of key exam points for each region is summarized here.

Hand Examination

Inspection: look for normal alignment of the fingers and record any abnormalities. Bony enlargement of the DIP (Heberden's nodes) (*Fig. 1*) and PIP (Bouchard's nodes) (*Fig. 2*) joints are classic for OA, and can be recognized immediately. Swan neck (*Fig. 3*) and Boutonniere (*Fig. 4*) deformities are seen in inflammatory arthropathies.

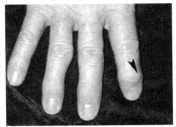

Figure 1

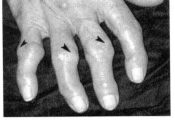

Figure 2

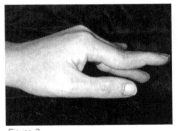

Figure 3

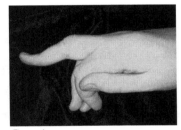

Figure 4

Mallet finger deformities (*Fig. 5*) can result from trauma or from inflammatory arthritis. The presence of nail pits is strongly associated with psoriatic arthritis.

Palpation: Be comfortable with the four-finger technique for finger joint evaluation (*Fig. 6*).

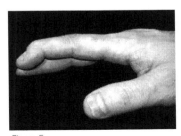

Figure 5

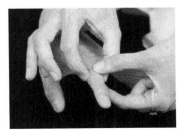

Figure 6

If the joint is enlarged, palpation should confirm for you whether the enlargement is from new bone formation, from excess fluid in the joint, or from thickening of the synovium. Bony enlargement will have the same texture and feel as the bridge of your nose; excess fluid will feel as if you were squeezing a grape, (the four finger technique provides maximum sensitivity) and thickened synovium (from hypertrophy, hyperplasia or tumor of synovium) will be similar in feel to pressing your finger against your own cheekbone-soft, but hard underneath.

Range of Motion: Normal fingers can tuck fully into a "karate chop" pose, with all finger pads in contact with the palmar surface of the corresponding MCP joint; and make a fist, which requires full flexion of the MCP joints. If there is no restriction in doing either of these two maneuvers, there is no significant abnormality in the DIP, PIP or MCP joints. If the patient is unable to do these maneuvers, you must assess passive range of motion of the affected fingers.

Special Tests: Nil are required for the core curriculum.

Wrist Examination

Inspection: View ulnar, radial, palmar and dorsal views. Look for swelling, erythema, deformity. Swellling over the radial aspect of the joint is nearly always due to osteoarthritic change in the thumb carpal-metacarpal joint, or from tenosynovitis of the extensor pollicus brevis and abductor pollicus longus tendons (DeQuervain's tendons). Swelling over the ulnar aspect of the wrist in the absence of trauma is very specific for inflammatory joint disease. The common extensor tendon sheath of the 2nd - 5th fingers is frequently swollen in rheumatoid arthritis; with finger extension the synovium buckles and "tuck sign" is apparent (*Fig. 7*).

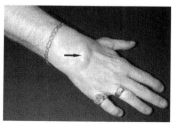

Figure 7

Palpation: Check for increased heat, making sure to compare to muscle, not tendon. Identify the ulnar styloid, radial tubercle, scaphoid and pisiform. At the base of the 2nd and 3rd metacarpals and just distal to the radial tubercle, there is normally an indentation where the proximal carpal row is easily palpable. If the wrist is swollen, fullness will be appreciated in this region.

Range of motion: Flexion, extension, radial and ulnar deviation, pronation and supination should be checked. The elbow must be held in 90° flexion to eliminate humeral contribution.

Special Tests: Phalen's (*Fig. 8*), Tinel's (*Fig. 9*) signs for median nerve compression and Finkelstein's tests for De Querrain's tenosynovitis are well described in all the standard textbooks, and should be reviewed and learned.

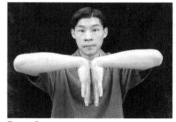

Figure 8   *Figure 9*

Elbow Examination

Inspection: The patient should be standing, if possible, for this part of the examination. Note the carrying angle, the presence of any nodules and bursal swelling over the olecranon process.

Palpation: Check for heat over the extensor surface of the joint. Identify the bony landmarks: medial and lateral epicondyles, radial head and olecranon. Palpate the olecranon bursa for swelling and the presence of nodules. Assess the joint for effusion; the normal recesses between the olecranon and epicondyles are lost when excess fluid is present in the joint.

Range of Motion: Flexion, extension, pronation and supination are the movements to be checked. Remember to assess pronation and supination with the elbow at 90° flexion.

Special Tests: Utilize the principle of stretch and stress to test for medial and lateral epicondylitis (Golfer's and Tennis elbow respectively). ie. Resisted extension of wrist produces pain from lateral epicondylitis, resisted palmar flexion of wrist produces pain from medial epicondylitis.

Shoulder Examination

The shoulder exam involves three synovial joints: sternoclavicular, acromioclavicular and glenohumeral; and one articulation: scapulo-thoracic articulation. The complete shoulder examination requires evaluation of all components.

Inspection: Compare both shoulders. Swelling of the shoulders may be subtle with loss of the pectoral-deltoid groove the only visible sign. Large joint effusions may cause the shoulder to look globally enlarged.

Palpation: Ask the patient where their shoulder pains and palpate this area last. Identify the spine of the scapula, the posterior and anterior edges of the acromion, the acromio-clavicular joint and the sternoclavicular joint. Check for tenderness at the insertion of the rotator cuff tendons, identify the bicipital groove and the long head of the biceps.

Range of Motion: Full active, unrestricted and unprotected movement of the shoulders effectively rules out significant pathology in the shoulder joints and no more testing is required in that instance. Ask the patient to bring their hands behind their head, then down behind their back, forward and up over their head, then slowly down to their sides. If there is hesitation or restriction of any movements, do them passively. Look for early scapulothoracic movement i.e. shrugging of the shoulder with abduction and flexion; this is a sign of glenohumeral disease.

Special Tests: The principle of putting tendons under stretch and stress is put to excellent use in the shoulder exam. Stretch the bicipital tendons by extending the shoulder and elbow, flexing the wrist and pronating the forearm. Stress the bicipital tendon by resisting its primary movements, i.e. shoulder and elbow flexion, wrist supination. Similarly test the rotator cuff tendons by resisting shoulder external and internal rotation and abduction. The supraspinatus can be simultaneously stretched and stressed by resisting upward movement of the internally rotated, abducted and forward flexed shoulder (*Fig. 10*). The acromioclavicular joint can be palpated for tenderness, and stressed by adducting the flexed shoulder and elbow across the chest (*Fig. 11*).

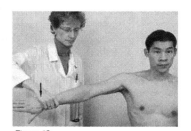

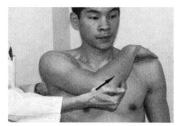

Figure 10

Figure 11

Cervical Spine

Inspection: Observe the position of the head relative to the neck and torso; is it held chin forward, is there marked upper thoracic kyphosis affecting head and neck position?

Palpation: In the screening exam, this can be skipped.

Range of Motion: Chin up, chin down, looking to the left and right, ear to shoulder movement should be observed. If there is restriction, assess passive range with the patient supine and with gentle movements to see if range can be incresed.

Special Tests: Deep tendon reflexes of the upper and lower extremity and Babinsky's test should be included in the screening rheumatologic exam.

Thoracic Spine

Inspection: Note shape of chest and deformities if present.

Palpation: As in cervical spine, in the sceening exam this can be skipped.

Range of Motion: Not required in the screening exam.

Special Tests: In patients with suspected or confirmed spondyloarthropathies, measure chest expansion. Use a tape measure at the nipple line, and measure from end expiration to maximum inspiration. Normal chest expansion is 5 cm.

Lumbar Spine/Sacroiliac Joints (see also *Approach to Back Pain*)

Inspection: Look for presence or absence of lumbar lordosis, café au lait spots, patches of hair. Identify the dimples of Venus and draw an imaginary line between them to get an idea about leg length discrepancy or pelvic obliquity from scoliosis.

Palpation: Skip this step in the screening exam. In the workup of the patient with back pain, lie the patient prone and palpate for tenderness of the muscles, spinous processes and SI joints. Use common sense; this would not be done in someone suspected of having a fracture.

Range of Motion: Flexion, extension and side flexion can be done with the patient standing. If side flexion is restricted, measure the distance between the tip of the long finger and the fibular head. Observe rotation with the patient sitting so as to fix the pelvis.

Special Tests: You should be comfortable with these named tests: Schober or a modified Schober (*Fig. 12*), Trendelenburg (*Fig. 13*), and Gaenslen (*Fig. 14*).

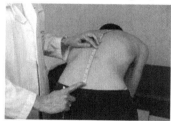

Figure 12

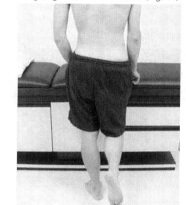

Figure 13

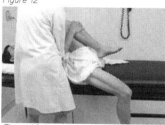

Figure 14

FABER tests: *(Fig. 15)* Pressure is applied downward through the flexed, externally rotated hip and through the opposite iliac crest. Pain may be elicited in the SI joint (buttock) or in the groin (hip) with this maneuver.

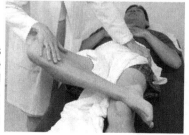

Figure 15

Straight leg raising, both sitting and lying, and deep tendon reflexes of the lower extremity round out the exam.

Hips

Inspection: Look for abnormal gait pattern, such as limp, trunk shift, lurch and decreased stance time in one or both legs.

Palpation: Once again not necessary on a screening examination, but in the patient with hip region pain, palpate the greater trochanter, anterior and posterior iliac crests and spines.

Range of Motion: Check internal and external rotation, abduction, adduction, flexion and extension. If the movements produce pain, make note of its location. Groin pain is in keeping with hip joint pain, but pain over the side of the hip or buttocks is more in keeping with pain from the lumbar spine, SI joints or trochanteric bursa.

Special Tests: Trendelenburg and FABER tests as in the lumbar spine/SI joint section. To test for hip flexion contracture, observe the position of the hip when lumbar lordosis is eliminated (Thomas test, *Fig. 16*).

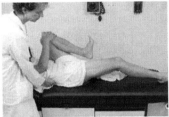

Figure 16

Knees

Inspection: Varus and valgus deformities, flexion contractures and "sway back knees" (genu recurvatum) should be looked for in the standing patient. Observe gait.

Palpation: Check for heat, swelling, tenderness and crepitus. Identify the joint line, patella and bursae.

Range of Motion: Flexion and extension are the primary movements of the knee. Tibial inversion and eversion should also be assessed in the flexed knee.

Special Tests: Look for small effusions by checking for bulge sign (*Fig, 17*). Large effusions are ballotted.

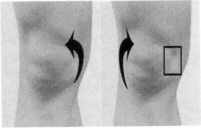

Figure 17

Test for ligamentous integrity by applying a stretching force to the 4 main ligaments in turn i.e. a valgus force to stetch the medial collateral ligament, a varus force for the lateral collateral ligament (*Figs. 18, 19 respectively*)

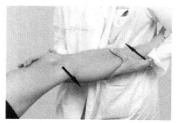

Figure 18

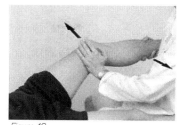

Figure 19

and pulling and pushing forces for the ACL (*Fig.* 20) and PCL respectively.

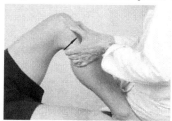

Figure 20

Ankle and Foot

Inspection: As with the other weight bearing joints, initial inspection should be with the patient standing. Look for signs of pain on walking with heel strike, plantar flexion and toe off. The medial malleolus should be higher than the lateral malleolus. Inspect the Achilles tendon for its integrity, nodule formation and alignment. Note alignment abnormalities of the forefoot and for preservation of the longitudinal arch. Look for splaying of the toes, a sign of MTP joint swelling. Examine the sole of the foot.

Palpation: Evaluate the ankle and foot much as you would the wrist and hand. Identify the important bony landmarks: medial and lateral malleoli, navicular, talus, calcaneus, base of the 5th metatarsal and the MTP joints. Check for tenderness, warmth and swelling in the ankles, mid-feet, MTP and IP joints of the toes.

Range of Motion: The true ankle joint has only two movements: dorsi- and plantar-flexion. This is best observed with the knee flexed so as to relax the gastrocnemius muscles. Next check inversion and eversion of the mid and fore foot. If active range is restricted, assess passive movement. Toe movement of flexion, extension, abduction and adduction are next assessed, keeping in mind the tremendous genetic variability in toe abduction and adduction. The sub-talar joint can only be assessed by passive range of motion; grasp the calcaneus by cupping the heel, lock the tibio-talar joint in dorsiflexion and apply varus and valgus forces. Normally there should be little movement with this maneuver.

Special Tests: Plantar fasciitis is common in the seronegative arthropathies and should be checked in patients with complaints of heel and foot pain. Grasp the heel and apply firm pressure distal/medial aspect of the calcaneus to see if pain is elicited. Stretch the plantar fascia by forcibly extending the toes (*Fig. 21*).

Figure 21

Figures in this chapter have been used with permission from:

A Primer on Musculoskeletal Examination. Sutton E., Novont Health Publishing Ltd., Halifax 2004.

[Section 7]
Joint Aspiration and Injection Techniques

[18] Approach to Joint Aspiration and Injection

Dr. D. Choquette, University of Montreal
& Dr. Lori Albert, University of Toronto

Indications for aspiration of joints and soft tissue

- ▶ Mandatory if septic arthritis is suspected
    - ⇉ Serial aspirations may be required to determine response to therapy
- ▶ Advised if crystal arthritis or hemarthrosis suspected
- ▶ To clarify diagnosis of arthritis as inflammatory vs non-inflammatory

Therapeutic indications

- ▶ Drainage of tense effusion to relieve pain and reduce intra-articular pressure
- ▶ Drainage of blood and purulent joint effusions
- ▶ Injection of corticosteroid

Contraindications to aspiration

Absolute:

- ▶ Suspected infection or open lesion on overlying skin or soft tissues

Relative:

- ▶ Bleeding diathesis
- ▶ Thrombocytopenia
- ▶ Prosthetic joint

Contraindications to injection

Absolute:

- ▶ Suspected infection of joint
- ▶ Bacteremia
- ▶ Prosthetic joint

Relative:

► Bleeding diathesis
► Thrombocytopenia
► Failure to respond to previous injections

Risks

► Hemorrhage into joint space
► Joint injury- may avoid by advancing needle slowly and preventing excessive movement of the needle while in the joint space
► Iatrogenic septic arthritis (RARE! <1:10,000)
► Tendon rupture (if corticosteroid injected directly into tendon)
► Subcutaneous fat atrophy and depigmentation of skin overlying injection site
► Cartilage injury with repeated injection (limit injections to 3/joint/year)

Procedure

1. Gather materials required

► Full sterile set up is not required as long as the operator is comfortable and the skin around the injection site will not be touched

Skin preparation:

► proviodine solution
► alcohol swabs
► sterile gauze pads
► local anaesthetic (1% lidocaine)
► sterile gloves
► Bandaid

Syringes and needle

► 21/22 gauge bore needle for non-septic aspiration. May require 18 gauge for septic fluid
► 3-5 cc syringes for diagnostic purposes, may use larger syringes for therapeutic drainage

Specimen collection

► Sterile specimen container/tube (without anticoagulant) for culture
► Tube with anticoagulant for cell count

Corticosteroid preparation

Please see chapter 12 (Approach to Therapeutics)

▶ Lidocaine: may be injected into the joint prior to or mixed with corticosteroid to ensure good placement and to provide immediate relief of pain

2. Landmark

▶ Critical to a successful procedure (see pictures below)
▶ Mark entry point with pen (may be erased by cleaning skin) or by creating an indentation in the skin with the tip of the needle cap, closed retractable pen, fingernail etc.

3. Sterilize the field

▶ Sterilize the field with 3 concentric outward spirals with iodine disinfectant (can use betadine soaked gauze- ensure non-sterile goves do not touch the field). Allow to dry.
▶ Use alcohol (can use swabs, ensuring that non-sterile gloves do not touch the field) to remove betadine from entry point.

You may check your landmark at this point if wearing sterile gloves. Otherwise, a fresh alcohol swab may be placed over the entry site and the non-sterile glove can palpate through the swab to check the land-mark (remove swab before introducing the needle).

4. Proceed with aspiration /injection (see pictures below)

Local anaesthetic may be used, but should be avoided if aspirating fluid for culture, as it may potentially interfere with the culture

Skin should be punctured quickly and then proceed more slowly toward the joint space, aspirating as you go. As soon as synovial fluid is obtained, avoid further forward movement of the needle to prevent dam-age to the cartilage.

If fluid is obtained initially and then flow stops:

▶ Ensure surrounding musculature is relaxed (especially for knee aspirations)
▶ Reposition the needle in small increments - release the suction initially (synovium may have been drawn up against the bevel of the needle), reposition gently, then attempt to aspirate again
▶ Re-inject some of the fluid in the syringe to relieve a poten-

tial blockage in the needle
► Apply counter pressure from another area of the joint to "push" fluid toward the needle

Once the syringe is full, disconnect syringe from the barrel of the needle and expel contents of this first aspirate into the sterile specimen container for culture. Re-attach this syringe (as long as it is uncontaminated) or a fresh one for further aspiration.

Placing a small sterile gauze over the barrel of the needle will improve your grip of the barrel and assist in detaching the syringe. This also keeps the exposed part of the needle sterile in case you have to advance the needle later on (some people also use a small hemostat or clamp). Do this part of the procedure slowly and carefully to avoid inadvertently repositioning the needle which may cause pain or cause synovial fluid flow to stop.

Aspirate as much fluid as possible without causing patient discomfort or repeated repositioning of the needle.

If corticosteroid is to be injected, attach the syringe containing corticosteroid to the barrel of the needle. Aspirate again to ensure that there is free flow of synovial fluid into the syringe before proceeding with injection. There should be minimal resistance to injection of the corticosteroid.

Corticosteroid injection should only be attempted if:

► There is no doubt that the needle is in the joint space
► Infection has been ruled out
► You first aspirate to ensure the needle tip is not in a blood vessel
► There is minimal resistance to flow upon injecting

5. Post-injection care

► Apply pressure to site for a few minutes with a clean gauze
► Keep injection site clean and dry for 24 hours (to avoid introduction of bacteria)
► Ideal to rest the injected joint for 24-48 hours
► Ice packs, acetaminophen, NSAIDS may relieve local pain

Post-injection flare: Patient may experience increased pain/burning in the joint beginning several hours after the injection. This is thought to be due to crystallization of the steroid preparation in the joint with secondary inflammation. This may last for 1-2 days and is self-limited. It can be treated with local application of cold and oral acetaminophen. Warn the patient that this may occur. However, any post-injection flare that persists or starts late requires attention.

6. Specific joint injections

Specific joint injections are best learned by observation of an experienced operator doing the procedure followed by performing the technique yourself under supervision. However, the following pictures and descriptions will assist you in learning these procedures.

1. Knee aspiration/injection

This is one of the simplest joints to access. There are several possible approaches. The medial and lateral approaches are most commonly used. In these approaches the knee is kept fully extended. The needle is inserted about 1/3 of the way down from the superior pole of the patella and directed perpendicular to the skin (direct the needle slightly inferiorly as the patellar undersurface slopes inferiorly). This can be done from the medial or the lateral aspect of the joint (see Figure 1 for medial approach). You should be able to palpate the space with your finger when landmarking. Note that there is greater muscle bulk on the medial aspect but the joint capsule is tougher laterally.

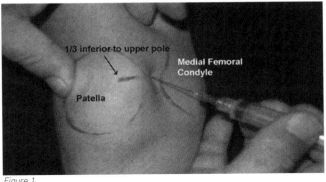

Figure 1

2. Shoulder injection

Once again, there are several approaches to the shoulder injection/aspiration. Glenohumeral joint aspiration may be difficult. If fluid cannot be obtained in the setting of an acute shoulder, radiologically guided aspiration is indicated (fluoroscopic or ultrasound guided).

Posterior approach: The patient is sitting. Palpate the posterior margin of the acromion and locate the most posterior and lateral point (the posterior "corner"). Insert the needle 1 cm below and 1 cm medial to this point, aiming slightly medially towards the coracoid process. The needle should be inserted until bone is touched.

Anterior approach: The patient is again sitting. The arm should hang at the side with the elbow flexed to 90°.Palpate the coracoid process and insert the needle 1 cm lateral and 1 cm distal to this point. The needle can be directed in a slightly upward direction. This approach is associated with a higher risk of vasovagal syndrome. Inserting the needle medial to the coracoid process may bring the needle into contact with neurovascular structures.

Subacromial bursa injection: This is used in the setting of subacromial impingement and some cases of calcific tendonitis. In this setting, injection of a mixture of lidocaine and corticosteroid is used, as relief of pain confirms the diagnosis. In this approach the patient is sitting. It is helpful to have adequate muscle relaxation to palpate the gap between the acromion and the humeral head. Insert the needle laterally under the acromion aiming slightly anteromedially (see Figure 2). There should be easy flow of fluid.

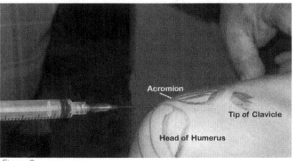

Figure 2

3. Ankle aspiration/injection

Injection or aspiration of the tibiotalar joint is accomplished with the patient in the supine position and the foot at a 90° angle with the leg. You can locate the joint line by gently flexing and extending the foot. The needle is inserted vertically into the joint space just medially to the tibialis anterior tendon and laterally to the medial malleolus (see Figures 3 & 4).

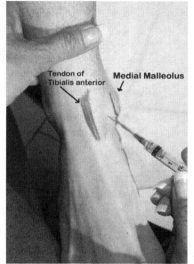

Figure 3

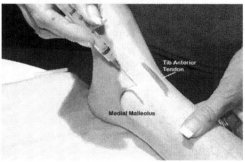

Figure 4

REFERENCES

Kelley's Textbook of Rheumatology, 7th ed., Harris ED, Jr, Budd RC, Firestein GS, et al, (Eds). WB Saunders, Philadelphia 2005.

Rheumatology, 3rd ed., Hochberg MC, Silman AJ, Smolen JS, Weinblatt ME, Weisman MH, (Eds). Mosby, St. Louis 2003

Primer on the Rheumatic Diseases, 12th ed., Klippel JH ed. Altlanta, USA: Arthritis Foundation, 2001

Up to Date©

[Section 8]
Checklist and Personal Case Log

RESIDENT'S CHECKLIST

Physical Exam (preceptored)

- ☐ GALS _____
- ☐ knee _____
- ☐ shoulder _____
- ☐ hand/wrist _____
- ☐ ankle/foot _____
- ☐ lumbar spine _____
- ☐ hip _____
- ☐ other _____

Injections / Aspirations (preceptored)

- ☐ knee _____
- ☐ shoulder _____
- ☐ ankle _____
- ☐ wrist _____
- ☐ other _____

Cases Seen

- ☐ Monoarthritis _____
- ☐ Undifferentiated Polyarthritis _____
- ☐ Rheumatoid Arthritis _____
- ☐ Gout _____
- ☐ Seronegative Spondyloarthropathy _____
- ☐ Lupus _____
- ☐ Myositis _____
- ☐ Raynaud's Phenomenon _____
- ☐ Vasculitis _____
- ☐ Osteoarthritis _____
- ☐ Back Pain _____
- ☐ Osteoporosis _____

Emergencies

- ☐ Septic Arthritis _____
- ☐ Temporal Arteritis _____
- ☐ Pulmonary Renal Crisis _____
- ☐ Scleroderma Renal Crisis _____

Therapeutic Experience

- ☐ NSAIDs _____
- ☐ Prednisone _____
- ☐ Colchicine _____
- ☐ Allopurinol _____
- ☐ Methotrexate _____
- ☐ Azathioprine _____
- ☐ Plaquenil _____
- ☐ Cyclophosphamide _____
- ☐ Salazopyrine _____

CANADIAN RESIDENTS' RHEUMATOLOGY HANDBOOK

CANADIAN RESIDENTS' RHEUMATOLOGY HANDBOOK

CANADIAN RESIDENTS' RHEUMATOLOGY HANDBOOK

CONTRIBUTORS

Lori Albert MD, FRCPC* (Editor)
Division of Rheumatology,
University Health Network, Toronto
Assistant Professor of Medicine,
University of Toronto

Volodko Bakowsky, MD, FRCPC
Division of Rheumatology
QEII Health Sciences Centre, Halifax
Assistant Professor of Medicine
Dalhousie University

Michael G. Blackmore MD, FRCPC
Affiliate, Division of Rheumatology
Sunnybrook and Women's College
Health Sciences Centre, Toronto
Instructor, Faculty of Medicine,
University of Toronto

Denis Choquette MD, FRCPC
Insitut de Rhumatologie de Montréal
Hôpital Notre-Dame
Université de Montréal

Paul Davis, MB,ChB,FRCP(UK),FRCPC
Associate Dean and Professor of Medicine,
University of Alberta

Avril A Fitzgerald MD, FRCPC
Associate Professor of Medicine,
Program Director Rheumatology,
University of Calgary
Chair RCPS(C) Specialty Committee in Rheumatology

Susan Humphrey-Murto, MD, FRCPC, MEd*
Division of Rheumatology
The Ottawa Hospital, Ottawa
Assistant Professor of Medicine,
University of Ottawa

Sharon A. Le Clercq MD, FRCPC
Associate Clinical Professor of Medicine,
University of Calgary

Heather McDonald-Blumer MD FRCPC
Division of Rheumatology
Mount Sinai Hospital, Toronto
Assistant Professor of Medicine,
University of Toronto

Janet Pope MD MPH FRCPC
Program Director, Rheumatology
St. Joseph's Health Care, London
Associate Professor of Medicine,
University of Western Ontario

Eric Rich MD, FRCPC*
Institut de Rhumatologie de Montréal
Hôpital Notre-Dame
Directeur de programme de Rhumatologie,
Université de Montréal

David B Robinson MD MSc FRCPC
Assistant Professor of Medicine,
University of Manitoba

Kam Shojania, MD, FRCPC*
Director, Clinical Trials, Arthritis Research Centre of Canada
Clinical Associate Professor of Medicine,
University of British Columbia

C. Douglas Smith, MD, FRCPC
Head, Division of Rheumatology,
The Arthritis Centre,
The Ottawa Hospital
University of Ottawa

Evelyn Sutton MD, FRCPC
Division of Rheumatology
QEII Health Sciences Centre, Halifax
Associate Professor of Medicine,
Program Director Rheumatology,
Dalhousie University

Recipient of a Clinician-Teacher Award from The Arthritis Society

ISBN 1-41205919-4

9 781412 059190

Edwards Brothers Malloy
Oxnard, CA USA
April 10, 2013